ONE WEE

Making your Way in Headship

Gerald Haigh
with Anne Perry

Routledge
Taylor & Francis Group

LONDON AND NEW YORK

First published 2008 by Routledge
2 Park Square, Milton Park, Abingdon, Oxon, OX14 4RN

Simultaneously published in the USA and Canada
by Routledge
280 Madison Ave, New York, NY 10016

Routledge is an imprint of the Taylor & Francis Group, an informa business

Typeset in AdobeGaramond by RefineCatch Limited, Bungay, Suffolk
Printed and bound in Great Britain by TJ International Ltd, Padstow,
Cornwall

British Library Cataloguing in Publication Data
A catalogue record for this book is available from the British Library

Library of Congress Cataloging in Publication Data
A catalog record for this book has been requested

ISBN 10: 1–84312–435–1
ISBN 13: 978–1–84312–435–1

Contents

Acknowledgements

I'm a 'former head teacher'. There are a lot of us about. We feel that somewhere inside us is a wealth of experience we can share, of children, teachers, advisers, officers, parents, governors, caretakers, plumbers . . . well, just of life really. That's probably true, but it's also undeniable that we very quickly get out of date. Headship today is different from what it was even five years ago. '

That's why I couldn't have done this book without the help of Anne Perry, Head of St Giles Junior in Warwickshire, who's been a key contributor of ideas all the way through. (She's very much a participant in the book, which is why her name is on the cover, although I take author's responsibility for what appears on the pages.)

Anne is a serving primary head, grappling every working day – and beyond – with all of the issues we touch on here, and more. She won't mind me saying that at the time of writing she's still pretty new in the job – though it's a sign of the times that her work's already been well-scrutinised by both Ofsted and the local authority.

That newness is an asset here. It means that the transition from deputy to head, and the challenges of the early months are still very fresh in her mind. As a head teacher and a busy wife, and mother of a primary school child, she's very much in touch with the realities of school life.

Much of what you read here started from conversations with Anne. Some of the rest is from my own experience. And there's a lot, too, that comes from the very many school visits I've made, and the conversations I've had through many years of visiting and writing about schools mostly for *The Times Educational Supplement* but also for *Guardian Education* and for a range of other newsletters, websites and professional journals. The more of that I do, the more I'm filled with admiration for the work being done by teachers, heads and support staff, and the more enjoyment I find in their good humour and wisdom. Most of all, though, I grow increasingly aware of the way that well led schools are bringing out the best in our young people. To walk a school with an excellent head who's sharing jokes with the children, returning greetings, giving encouragement is to know that to be a head teacher is to be in a special and privileged place, charged with the care of all our futures.

I'm indebted to many colleagues, many of whose experiences are used here, to local authority officers in Warwickshire, and particularly to Mark Eales of Doncaster authority, whose wise ideas on headship have been enormously helpful to me.

Introduction

The title of 'teacher' is a proud one, revered in every civilisation since the dawn of human history. That's because teachers carry the most important responsibility of all, that of nurturing the young people who will in the fullness of time take humanity forward. It follows that to be a head teacher is to be doubly privileged, because it carries the opportunity not only to shape the life chances of very many young people, but to be a guide and mentor for the teachers themselves as they grow in professionalism and responsibility.

That teaching isn't always perceived in this way, and that it's consequently becoming more difficult to persuade teachers to become heads is an indictment of the way that our nation sees its schools and the education of its children. It's become difficult for teachers and heads to maintain a sense of vocation and of commitment to the emotional and creative growth which form the core of true education.

We'd maintain, though, that all of this makes it more important, not less, that good teachers become heads. Look around and you'll find that there are many head teachers who enjoy and relish their work, who maintain a sense of mission and who know the real and deep satisfaction of seeing young people discover themselves and the world beyond, and of helping teachers to grow in wisdom as well as in classroom technique. You will hear many heads who will say, unprompted, without irony or affectation, 'It's the best job in the world.'

There's always lots to learn about headship of course. That's why we've written this book. Not to delve too deeply into the philosophy of leadership – there's hardly space to do that. No, our purpose is to deal with some of the knots and snags and practicalities. Maybe you won't always agree with the solutions we've offered, but at least we'll help you to think again about your own way of doing things. And if you're already doing what we've suggested, why then maybe we've given a little reassurance.

If you're not a head yet, then we hope you're going to get there. What we say to you is that if you're a good teacher it's never too early to start thinking about the route to headship. It's your natural goal. Don't be put off by thoughts of how difficult it is or by talk of paperwork and responsibility. If you can run a class, keeping 30 children, all different, all lively, all demanding, moving forward in good order, and still have time to enjoy their company then you may not recognise it but you're already working a small, daily miracle. So be certain that if you can do that, then with the right experience and help you'll be able to run a school. And when you get there, you'll find that being a good, successful head teacher arms you with more than enough confidence and assurance to see off any unpleasantness that comes your way.

Earlier, we mentioned the double privilege of headship – that of being mentor both to young people and to teachers. There is, though, a third privilege. To be a head is to be part of a wonderful, mutually supportive community of professionals. You don't know until you join them just how selfless, helpful, irreverent and full of fun is a close-knit community of local head teachers, united in understanding, vocation and vision. If you're there already, you know how true that is. If you're thinking of joining, then don't hesitate. It really is the best club in the world.

Prologue
The big one

In this profession of ours, promotion tends to come in small steps. Some of them, indeed, are financially invisible.

> *'John, I know you've enough to do already, but now Margaret's gone off to run assessment at Grunge Street, we're really stuck on the humanities front. I wonder, just till we get ourselves sorted out . . .?'*

Poor John might not see that as promotion. He may feel it's more of an extra burden, with no extra money. On the other hand, it's a clear sign that he's trusted, and it'll read well on his CV. So he takes it on.

So, gradually, John – like Margaret, who's gone on to an assistant headship – works his way upwards, sometimes seeing a little more money, sometimes not, always taking on more responsibility, occasionally moving to another school.

Each new job – some more than others – feels a bit different. There are new people, different children, other duties. Cut to the essentials though and when it comes down to it, each new teaching job is actually very much like the last one. There's teaching to do, an area of school life to look after and a head teacher who's setting the pace. That's what it's like as you move up the ladder. Even being a deputy head isn't really all that different. In the primary sector you'll have a significant teaching timetable with, as often as not, responsibility for a class. So there you are, with years of experience, on top of the job, a confident teacher, able to carry responsibility.

Then comes the big one, your own headship, and suddenly the landscape changes.

Moving to a different planet

Any head will tell you that the move to headship isn't just another promotion. It's a step into another order of reality altogether. Here's a real head, a few months into the job, talking about it.

> *'I want to emphasise that nothing – but nothing – can really prepare you for what it feels like to be a head. Don't get me wrong. In all sorts of ways I was well trained. When I was a deputy my head included me in everything. I shared a room with her. I ran the school when she was ill. I went on the courses. But I tell you that the reality doesn't hit you till you're actually the person in charge, the one who's supposed to know.'*

Here's someone else on the same theme.

> *'On my first day, I was at school before anyone else. I said hello to the caretaker and then I walked around the building for half an hour as people arrived. It sounds foolish to say it, but only gradually did it sink in that I wasn't a visitor, and that everyone else who arrived was actually waiting for me to say or do something. The whole place was focussed on me. That's when it struck me that I was now the boss.'*

Is it a good feeling? Of course it is – these are people who've finally landed the job they've always wanted. It's a heady sensation, driven by the realisation that this is the biggest job in the most rewarding of all professions. That moment, as you walk round your school on your first day, is the one you've been waiting for all your professional life. How can we help you to get there? How can we help you to deal with it when you arrive? How can we help you to reflect on the way you're doing it right now? Our task, as colleagues who have trodden the road already, is to share our experience with you – not to give you all the answers, because in the end you'll find them for yourself, but to provide some starting points, a lot of encouragement, a few tricks of the trade and perhaps a bit of inspiration.

Chapter 1
What's the head there for?

It's not really a silly question. Try it on any serving primary head and you'll hear, straight back without a second's hesitation, 'You might well ask!'

Consider, for example, the 'fortnight-off' test. It goes like this. Ask yourself, and others in your school, this question. If every adult in the average primary school took two weeks off in turn, whose absence would call for the least amount of forward planning, and cause the minimum of inconvenience? Think about how it works.

- Class teacher away? Get on the phone to the supply agency pronto.

- Teaching assistant? Great! Just my luck. I've got to reorganise my whole programme.

- School administrator? Help! There's dinner money coming in, and the phone's ringing.

- Caretaker? There were windows left open overnight. The cleaners are mutinying. A toilet's blocked.

- Head teacher? How long did you say she'd been away?

Good knockabout stuff isn't it? But what it does is focus the mind on the fact that the head's primary role is to do with strategic leadership – with having a clear vision of what his/her school should be, can be and will be, and successfully selling that vision to the whole of the school community and beyond. Selling it, moreover, to such effect that everyone believes it possible, and becomes determined to see it become reality.

'Selling' – just before you leap in to criticise the word – admittedly isn't quite right. It implies that only you have the vision, and that you can implant it, intact, into vacant spaces in other people's minds. 'Releasing' is nearer because the people around you have their own ideas, motives and ambitions waiting to be encouraged and brought into the mix. Then, of course, there's 'Developing', because you can't just throw the ingredients in and let them stew.

There for the long haul

This is as good a point as any, I suppose, to emphasise – and it won't be for the first time – that to be a successful head teacher is to play a long game. (Which is why the head can be away for two weeks without anyone really noticing.) High standards which are robust and deeply ingrained in the school culture take time to achieve. Winning colleagues over, building them into a team isn't an overnight job. And the curve of improvement isn't a steady upward slope. At times it's flat. It may even dip.

Staff changes

The most common cause of a dip in a school's improvement march is the loss of key members of staff. In a good school, teachers want to move on, and it's the head's duty and privilege to help them to do so. But the effect on the school can be profound. The lesson is that the recruitment and retention of good teachers is always going to be a very high priority for you. Don't neglect it. Keep looking ahead, keep spotting good people – students on school experience.

A head says,

> *In my first year of headship, as we were working hard to move out of special measures, three key members of staff left. Recruitment is always difficult here, and inevitably we were into a long period of supply cover and temporary appointments. I cannot emphasise too much how easily a strongly improving school can be knocked by something like this.'*

So, there'll be times for courage and steadfastness. Just never forget that all the old sayings, including 'Rome wasn't built in a day' have become clichés because they are true.

■ But it's not only strategy

The strategic role, then, is the most important. But it can't be the only one. For a primary school child, passing through, with only one moment to seize, one bus to catch, the long-term vision doesn't really count. What he/she wants is the best possible deal right now. So for you, the head teacher, the challenge is to stick with the long view while at the same time making sure today's children are as well served as possible. Here's a head talking about that. He's not a primary head. In fact at the time he said this he was leading one of the biggest comprehensives in the country, with over 2000 pupils.

> *'I walk the whole of the school every day and I never ignore anything. If there's a child standing in the corridor in lesson time I want to know what they're doing. If there's noise coming from a room I find out whether it's the right kind of noise. If I find a smelly toilet I seek out the site supervisor and take it up with him. You might argue that there are others to whom this kind of thing is delegated and that by getting bogged down in trivialities I'm being distracted from strategic leadership. My answer is that these are not trivialities at all. Every small incident like that represents a step away from our shared vision. So, for instance, I do not want a school with smelly toilets, for example, because smelly toilets represent, to me, an unnecessary acceptance of poor standards. I don't know if you make wide-ranging snap judgements about places – hotels, restaurants, bus stations, factories – based on the condition of their toilets. I know I do. So they're worth my time and effort.'*

What we learn from this is that although there's an often frustrating round of day-to-day tasks to be done, and never enough time to stand back and see the big picture, the trick is to see each apparently small task for what it is – a signifier of something much more profound and strategic.

Chapter 2
Dealing with distractions

The screaming frustration caused by trying to keep focussed on what you've planned to do – next year, next term, tomorrow, in the next 10 minutes – is one of the first things you'll learn about headship. That's why we've put it in this early chapter. At its worst, the pressure of events leads you to forget what you're there for.

Other jobs suffer in the same way mind you. The National Health Service, bless it, is always good for a management story. Here's one from a head teacher. He calls it 'Spot the distraction'.

'I was in hospital, lying awake on the ward, as you do, in the early hours of the morning. Nearby, the nurse who seemed to be in sole charge of the ward was busy at a desk doing some paperwork and occasionally making phone calls to other departments. Further down the ward a restless patient called for her on two or three occasions – I couldn't hear what he wanted. Each time the nurse got up and trotted down the ward and back.

Eventually, on one of her visits to the patient, she raised her voice and I heard her say – and this is absolutely, hand-on-heart true – "You'll have to stop this. I'm trying to get on with my work".'

Florence Nightingale, I guess, could hardly have put it better.

The story is a sharp reminder that what you think of as distractions are often truly part of the job. So, for example, if you're trying to get a letter written and the phone rings, or one of your colleagues or a child pops in to see you, then you shouldn't be annoyed because the phone call and the visit are actually part of what you're there for.

▓ Does this mean there are no distractions?

It's certainly true that you have to guard against allowing your personal irritation at being interrupted to colour your reaction to a reasonable request. Your school administrator or secretary, after all, has to be an expert at multi-tasking, and there are heads who could learn from watching a good school secretary at work.

That said, yes, it's obvious that there really are interruptions that are unnecessary as well as unwelcome. Part of the problem is timing. Even something that legitimately demands your attention is a distraction if it arrives at the wrong time. In the early months of headship, you need to focus on some priorities, and demands outside those priorities can legitimately be called distractions. Here's a head recalling those early days.

> 'There was an induction process for new heads, and I could have been out of school on induction events for maybe 20 days in the first term. Then on top of that there's the stream of visitors. Everyone wants a piece of you – people from health and safety, and finance, for instance. Each one thinks their issue is the priority. They don't realise that they're only a part of the big picture and that you haven't got time to deal with it all at once.'

It's not difficult to see how this happens. Each local authority department is very keen that their new head doesn't make a fatal error – with finance, for example, or with health and safety – before they've had a chance to visit.

Some of these induction events and visits are useful and important. Others, frankly, are not. Here's another head.

> 'I went to new head induction events that had me jumping up and down with impatience. The priority for every new head is to be in school. So if we're taken out of school, we need to feel that we're being

*given the most important information quickly and efficiently. We
don't want light-hearted speeches about generalities. We don't want
leisurely buffet lunches. In many cases the most important bit of an
induction event is the chance to meet the key people at the office, and
to know which of them we should phone when we have a problem.
Anything else we can sort out as we go along.'*

Keeping focussed in the early days – key principles

For a head, nothing is a three-line whip. You have more clout and
independence than you think you have. If you want to say no to a
meeting with the Chief Officer, or to a visit by an adviser, then you can
certainly do so. Common courtesies, such as the offer of an alternative,
are important of course.

- Spread the distractions out – try not to be out of school twice in
the same week, and try to vary the days of the week.

- Put a time limit on visits. If it's a key visitor – your local inspector
for example – ask how long the visit will take and be prepared to
take the initiative in drawing it to a close when time's up. If it's a
less important visitor, set the time limit yourself, 'I can give you
half an hour . . .'.

- Don't be afraid to leave a course or a meeting if it's not working for
you. Try not to walk out in the middle of someone's presentation,
but do be prepared to leave between speakers or at coffee time. If at
the end of a long day you say, 'That was a waste of time,' then
frankly you shouldn't have stuck it out.

- At most induction events, the key question, to which you want to
write down the answer is, 'Who do I approach when I want to
know more about this? And what's the phone number?'

A head says,

'The theories of time management are fine, but the reality is very difficult to handle. At the end of one term at a very busy time, I'd organised a whole day around a case conference I'd been asked to attend out of school that was supposed to take place at 10 am. They changed it twice at the last minute, once to 12 o'clock and then to 2 pm – and I was having an assembly for staff who were leaving that afternoon. I suppose the obvious thing for me to do was tell them I couldn't come, but the truth is that the meeting did need to happen, and the end of term was coming up, so I just had to swallow the problems.'

Case conferences – meetings of concerned agencies about a child – are particularly demanding for primary heads. Our head goes on:

'You can take a whole day out on a child protection case – it's a lot of time to spend on one child out of the whole school. Then there's all the preparation that goes into it, the finding out of information. It's worth it if you get a result that's good for the child – if you see them getting support. But it's very demanding.'

■ A word about paper

'Paperwork' has become a word with negative vibes. Heads and teachers all complain of too much paperwork.

Really there are two main kinds of paperwork. There's the stuff that you have to generate in school – policies, curriculum plans, development plans, data of various kinds – and there's the blizzard that comes through the post.

There's no real way round the 'official' kind except to keep purely internal demands for paper to a minimum. Very detailed curriculum and lesson plans, for example, need to be carefully measured against the extent to which they're actually used by the people they're written for. Always ask whether it's necessary. Ask, 'Why are we doing this? Does it work towards improved teaching and learning?'

If, as a new head, you can remove some layers of paperwork early on, you'll win friends.

You should also make sure that ICT is used to the full for sharing lesson plans and ideas on the school network.

Beyond that, there's software around now that enables you to keep all of your policies and plans on a shared, web-based platform, accessible by staff from wherever they want to work. If you're a school that has to complete Ofsted's Self Evaluation Form (SEF), the same software will link all of your work to the SEF, enabling you to keep the Form under constant review as the year goes on. A head says,

> *'I used to have a line of box files on my shelf for policies and plans. Now they're all available to all of us on the web, for discussion and continuous review.'*

As for the stuff that comes in the post, a large part of the problem lies firmly at the door of the many agencies, organisations and businesses, from government down to the local pizza house, who think that schools represent a captive audience. Every day, the post brings a mountain of stuff that may or may not contain material that's important or interesting (few items, sadly, are both).

If you're not going to be overwhelmed, much of what comes in has to be filtered out. That's not easy. What looks like junk mail may well contain the germ of something intriguing. Charities, for example, will tell you that they're frustrated by the task of trying to get to head teachers who may well be interested in what they have to say and do. Really you have to decide whether you're just going to throw everything into the recycle bin, put it all into the staffroom unsorted or have a member of the support staff go through all of the non-essential post plucking out items that could be useful – a free offer, a worthy charity, an interesting school visit, a music workshop. . . .

■ Tidiness

Are you untidy? Do you have a desk piled up with paper? Has the paper migrated into piles against the walls? It's not as worrying as some management trainers seem to think. As Laurence J. Peter, an American educator, is reputed to have said,

'If a cluttered desk is a sign of a cluttered mind, of what, then, is an empty desk?'

An almost infinite number of things matter more than keeping your room and your desk tidy. The most important parts of your job happen in classrooms and corridors. So never, for example, apologise to a visitor for the state of your room. (Would you apologise for any other aspect of your work? 'So sorry I'm poor at monitoring teaching and learning. Aren't I awful?')

What matters is whether you can find the stuff you need when you need it. If you really feel you're drowning in paper, fetch your secretary in occasionally to work down the various piles with you, deciding what to throw away, what to deal with and what to put in a file somewhere.

You will certainly find official documents with reply deadlines that have already gone by. If you think you're losing out on something important to you, ring up and apologise – the deadlines are never all that firm. If it's something important to them, they'll ring you.

Chapter 3

Wading through treacle – more distractions

There are various levels of distraction. Long meetings and unwelcome visitors make up just one sort. There are also what we call 'micro-distractions' – the things that happen all the time to stop you just getting on. The best way to illustrate this is to describe the start of the day for one primary head.

- 08.10 Arrive in school. On your mind as you hurry from the car park is the realisation that you'll be taking assembly in an hour. You know what you're going to do in assembly, but first you have to do a few things. You need to go to a classroom to retrieve an excellent poem by one of the children from the wall where it's displayed, make an OHP transparency of it in on the photocopier in the staff workroom, get the projector to the hall and make sure it's working. And you've arrived 10 minutes later than you planned.

  But as you go through the door, the caretaker's waiting in the entrance hall to tell you there's a problem with the intruder alarm. It went off in the night, and he was called out by the police. Everything was fine, but the alarm wouldn't reset and it's going to need attention. The caretaker suspects the hanging mobiles in Year Three and wonders if you'd talk to the teacher about taking them down. He's a bit agitated by this and it takes him some time to get it all off his chest.

- 08.20 As you look at your watch and turn to go off to get the poem, the phone rings in the office. The secretary's not in yet so you pick up the call. It's Jack Johnson, husband of one of your teachers, and a friendly person well known to you. He wants to tell you that Mrs Johnson's ill and won't be in. As soon as you realise that, you want him off the phone so you can do something about finding a supply teacher. But he's in a chatty mood and it's a full 5 minutes before you get him off the phone so you can immediately speed dial the supply agency. They're excellent – quick on the uptake, and you're pretty sure they'll ring you back with a name within minutes.

■ 08.30 The secretary comes in. You brief her quickly about the burglar alarm and the supply agency, look at your watch, swear quietly and set off to get that poem. But as you pass the main door, a distinguished looking man in a suit with a briefcase – a bit like a retired officer in a fifties film – is buzzed in by the secretary. He looks important, and you think 'Ofsted!' so you pause to ask him if you can help. Big mistake. He's selling cheap carpet offcuts, and it takes another 5 minutes before you can disengage yourself.

■ 08.35 You're setting off on your tour again when the secretary puts her head out and calls you.
  'The vicar's on the phone!'

■ You've been trying to talk to the vicar all week. You're not a church school, but you're a new head and the vicar's an important local contact. So you sigh and go back to your office to take the call. You cut the call as short as you can by making a date for him to come and see you for a longer chat.

■ 08.45 You come out of your room and look at your watch. In 20 minutes time you'll be taking assembly. Is there now enough time to get that poem? It's worth a shot, so you half run down the corridor to the classroom where it's on the wall. The teacher's in there by now. She's ever so glad to have caught you. There's something really important she wants to discuss about one of the children in the class. . . .

■ 09.00 You head back to the photocopier, through corridors filled with smiling children who want to show you things and tell you their news. When you get to the copier there's a handwritten note sellotaped to it that says,

'Out of order. Somebody broke it and didn't tell anyone. Engineer coming this afternoon.'

■ 09.10 You're standing in the hall smiling at the children as they come in. Once again it's an autopilot assembly.

'Good morning children. I want to tell you about something that happened to me on my way to school today. . . .'

Is that a good start to the day? Be assured that plenty of heads have experienced something like it – and it's quite likely that you will too.

How, though, to avoid it? What could this head have done to make the start of the day a little better do you think?

■ Assembly

Assembly is an important part of school life, and deserves more, and earlier, thought than the head in our story was giving it. If our head really did get into this pickle, then it would have been better to drop the original assembly idea at an earlier stage and just reach for something to read aloud. Either that or there are some excellent 'pre-packaged' assemblies such as 'Primary Assembly File' from PfP publishing.

■ Arriving in the morning

Two things are always going to happen – maybe not every morning, but often enough to make it worth being ready for them.

1   On a day when you've planned to arrive early, you will, in fact, arrive late. If it's not your youngest throwing a tantrum, it'll be the traffic. And if it's neither of those, it'll be the disappearance of your school or car keys.

2   On a day when you're focussed on heading in and going straight to a planned job, there'll be a ready-made distraction waiting for you. And on at least a proportion of those of days, it'll be the caretaker, bearing ominous news.

All of which should be telling you that your school really needs to be well staffed from quite early in the morning. You'll find that there are times when important decisions have to be made during the hour or so before the children arrive. The clock ticks down to their arrival and there's serious stuff to be done.

So if you're going to be prepared for heating breakdowns, overnight burglaries, serious staff absence, severe weather – any of the eventualities that call for some quick decisions and follow-up action you must try not to be alone. That means:

■   having senior staff in early. You'll be setting an example yourself, of course, but it's reasonable to expect some senior support, from people taking it in turn to be in either with you or at least not far behind. If you can't make this work on an informal basis, then you might call it 'early duty' and balance it against other duties during and after the school day.

■   opening the admin department early. It's a really good idea to organise your admin staff so that someone's there early to take phone calls and handle visitors. Eight thirty, we think, isn't early enough. Lots happens before that in a busy school – staff are in, the head's in, parents and teachers are phoning. Eight fifteen is good. Eight o'clock is better. That doesn't mean you have to make your secretary work a longer day. What's needed is a flexible approach – a rota so that admin people take the 'early shift' in turn.

■ Reception

Run a good reception system, that's open well before school, and then let it take its course. If our head had let the receptionist speak to the posh visitor, and find out who he was, a lot of time would have been saved.

The vicar

The vicar problem is just one example of how a keen head can be distracted by his/her own personal priorities. The head in our story is keen to talk to the vicar, and that's important – but another day of waiting isn't going to matter. So why be distracted? To be fair, that sort of thing happens all the time. There you are, entirely focussed on an important task, when something attracts your attention, and before you have time to tune it out, you've swerved aside.

Here's another example. On your way to a pre-planned and well-prepared lesson observation, you put your head in to another teacher to check whether her whiteboard's now working properly. You realise she's covering a maths topic that you know a lot about, so you sidle into the room for a moment and before you know it, 15 minutes have gone by. The teacher waiting for your observation becomes increasingly annoyed as she tries to rein back the pace so that you won't miss her excellent introduction.

What's the answer? Just the obvious one really – you have to realise that although it's within the nature of human beings to wander through the countryside poking at the undergrowth and pausing to watch the upward flight of the skylark, life as a primary head just doesn't work like that. 'Eye on the ball' is as good a way of putting it as any other. At times this might mean cutting someone short, maybe slightly offending them. But that goes with the territory too.

Chapter 4

Delegation

One way of dealing with distractions is to use efficient delegation. That's why all of the time-management courses and books make much of the need to delegate. What they don't always take account of – especially if they're written for a general business readership – is that delegation poses particular problems for a primary head. The obvious difficulty is that in most primary schools, every teacher other than the head is busy all day with the children. Because classes can't be left to fend for themselves, the head is the only person able to move around responding to problems, to make uninterrupted phone calls or to see unexpected visitors in unhurried privacy.

It's really important, though, that you do not give up, stop trying to delegate and settle for just getting on and doing everything, perhaps with the help of a loyal and long-serving secretary. Typically, the head and secretary have offices next to each other, and a sort of head–secretary axis can grow up that seems to exclude other people, all of whom feel that their absorption in their classroom work cuts them off from whole-school decision-making.

■ Delegation is difficult but necessary

You just can't give up on your attempts to delegate. It's not just that you can't really do all the work effectively yourself. Good delegation in the primary school:

- is effective professional development for your colleagues
- gives colleagues insight into your motives and methods
- is good for staff team building
- is good for the school, because new people bring new skills and renewed enthusiasm.

However, delegation isn't just giving out jobs to other people. The culture has to be right first. If it's not, that's when you find people saying,

> *'I don't believe it. I'm up to my eyebrows already, and she's landed me with this.'*

Ideally, people take on additional work because:

- they have been convinced that they have the ability to do something important
- they know that carrying out the task will provide valuable professional development.

And money? Where does that come into this? Don't people complain if they're asked to do more work for the same money? Not, according to the research, in teaching. Money's nice, but it's not the main motivator. That said, it's good – and fair – when a head and governing body can offer more money to someone who takes on more work. (And we shouldn't forget that there are various flexible options for one-off payments. Talk to your authority's HR department about the ins and outs of this.) All the evidence is, though, that for teachers at least, money isn't the main motivator. Very often, quite a small, symbolic payment is hugely appreciated. It's the gesture that matters, and the recognition.

▉ The deputy head

The primary deputy has a difficult job. Invariably he/she teaches for much of the day, and frequently is actually a class teacher. The danger of that is that the head falls into 'do it all myself' mode, with the result that:

- the head's efforts are spread too thinly
- the deputy is not being properly prepared for headship
- the deputy is perceived by colleagues as an expensive class teacher.

Both head and deputy have to work hard to avoid this. If it's allowed to go on, it's demoralising for everyone as well as being a clear example both of inefficient management and of poor value for money. You as head have the main responsibility, with the governors, for giving the deputy time to contribute to school management, and the opportunity to observe and share in your work as the school's leader. This means having your deputy:

- understand and contribute to your own decision-making
- sometimes represent you at key meetings in and beyond school
- take a share of staff meetings and training sessions
- attend governors' meetings, contributing in discussion
- take assembly regularly
- be a very visible senior person, someone you take seriously and to whose views you will at times defer.

Consider moving your deputy to a desk in your own room. The chances are he/she won't be there for much of the time, but it's an excellent way of bolstering the deputy's role, and providing him/her with experience of the inner workings of leadership.

Other colleagues

1   Try to have key leadership figures out of the classroom for significant chunks of time. You need to be sure, of course, that their time is not only used well but is seen in that light by the rest of the staff. That's up to you and the team. But remember that nothing does more damage to management in any walk of life than

the perception that they swan around not doing very much, or are closeted away in meetings.

2   Get to know, in depth, the strengths and preferences of your colleagues. That means seizing opportunities to talk to them, individually, as often as possible. Don't be afraid to ask them what they would like to be doing in the school. Unearth the hidden ambitions. Find the person who is itching to reorganise the library but has never said so for fear of treading on toes. Or the teaching assistant who has the enthusiasm, skills and understanding to be an effective assistant to the learning support co-ordinator. Or the other teaching assistant who'd be happy to come early and be paid as a receptionist for the busy hour between eight and nine in the morning.

Chapter 5
Taking stock

You became a head because there are things you want to do that you couldn't do as a deputy or assistant head. As you came up the ladder you certainly collected responsibility, but that just made you want more, because as you drew nearer to headship, you began to think, 'I could do that'.

So, does a new head stand on the threshold of the school, hands rubbing together, saying, 'Right, it's time to get stuck in'?

Perhaps. But there are some notes of caution to bear in mind. Being a head isn't about satisfying your feeling that 'I could do that'. Nor is it about putting long-cherished, personal plans into action. The fact is that until you've been in the job for a while, you don't really know, in detail, what it is that you want to do. That's because you need to find out what the school needs first, and that can take a bit of time.

You may, of course, think some things are obvious. If the approach to the school is a sea of litter, then you may want that to disappear within the day. If the children are running riot, and the toilet doors have been kicked off their hinges, then that, too, is a state of affairs that begs for your attention.

That sort of short-term blitz hardly touches the overall strategy though. Once you've had the litter cleared up, and waded into some of the more immediate behaviour problems, then you still need to work patiently, over time, on the underlying reasons. And that's a task that begins with the gathering of information.

Information gathering

The great transformational leaders in all walks of life are, above all, collectors of information. They're people like Louis V. Gerstner, who transformed IBM from a moribund shadow of its former self into a rejuvenated powerhouse of an organisation. Gerstner worked himself to a frazzle in the early days, not by throwing his weight about and preaching the Gerstner way, but by being hungry for knowledge about what he'd come into. He travelled, observed, read reports, studied data and, above all, listened to people. Here he is, on his early days in the job:

> *In all the meetings over those several weeks, I was sizing up my team, trying to understand the problems they faced and how they were dealing with them, how clearly they thought, how well they executed and what their leadership potential really was.*

> (Gerstner 2002)

And this, remember, is someone facing a huge financial crisis that had to be dealt with in very short order. Despite that, Gerstner knew that he couldn't really move on with his senior people until he had the measure of them and until they trusted and knew him. One phrase in that extract resonates:

> '. . . *trying to understand the problems they faced and how they were dealing with them'.*

There could hardly be a better mission statement for the early months of headship. The head who, after half a term, can say,

> *'I have a good idea of the problems faced by my colleagues, and I know how they are dealing with them'*

is surely well on the road to success.

How do you achieve that sophisticated understanding of the institution you've taken on? You've done the obvious things long

before, of course, at the interview stage – read the Ofsted
reports, looked at the assessment data. Now you're embarking on
the job, though, you're going to be observing and listening, and
that involves meeting people and trying to see the school through
their eyes.

■ Meeting key people

When you're appointed to a headship, lots of people want to talk to
you. The chair of governors will want to take you on one side and
tell you the true story of the school and what it needs. Your deputy
head, and perhaps one or two other long-serving members of staff,
may want to do the same. The school administrator or secretary
may even try to get in on the act, in a discreet and correct way.
And, of course, your local authority adviser will have something to
say too.

It's really important that you give each of these people a fair chance
of meeting with you in a private and unhurried way. Before you start,
though, remember that each of them comes to you with a particular
agenda. The chair of governors represents the people who actually gave
you the job. They made the choice because they thought you had
particular qualities and abilities, and it's likely that he/she will want to
make sure that you've understood what their thinking is about the
school's future. The local authority is to some extent accountable for the
school's future performance – they certainly don't want you to fall at the
first Ofsted hurdle.

And the deputy and your other colleagues? They're undoubtedly
quite apprehensive, and much depends on what they thought of the
previous head. If, as is so often the case, your predecessor was revered
and renowned, then they're going to be worried that you'll change
things for the worse, perhaps throwing out valued traditions and
practices.

If, on the other hand, your predecessor wasn't well thought of – and
there are a whole lot of possible reasons for this, none of which we need
to explore here – then your colleagues may well be signalling that fact
to you.

▨ Running the early meetings

The key people for your first one-to-one meetings, either before you start or soon after, are your deputy head, the chair of governors, the site manager or caretaker and the senior admin officer or school secretary. Take care with the way you arrange your meetings. Give them equal time and consideration. Having to cancel or rearrange any of them will get you off on the wrong foot.

The length of the meetings is less important than the fact of having them, but 20 minutes to half an hour is about right. Don't give more time to one person than another – again it's a matter of the signals you're sending. You don't want the caretaker, for example, to feel marginalised into a brief and hurried session.

Whether you run these meetings formally or regard them as informal and freewheeling is up to you. Some advocate printing an agenda, with a space for notes. This clarifies things and signals that you are taking the meeting seriously. Others believe that colleagues are more easily drawn out if they're put informally at ease.

In each meeting, make sure your values, beliefs and expectations come across. Don't be afraid to prepare a little speech, just in case you think you're not being properly understood. You want people to go away clear about what you stand for.

Your deputy (and other senior colleagues)

They will want to tell you some of their woes. They may have had a difficult time – the last months of a headship, or a period of time with an acting head, can be very challenging, and your deputy may imply, or tell you outright, that you're going to have to get a grip of things. Listen carefully, make notes. It's best, though, not to engage directly with their worries – so don't say things like, 'Really! My word, I'd better tackle that straight away!' Better to respond with something like,

'I intend to work with you to decide on our priorities. What I ask of you, before we even start our journey together, is that I have your support and your loyalty. We won't always agree – we're all independently minded professionals, so it's inevitable that we'll have

our differences. I hope I'll always encourage you to speak up – but I expect you to do your protesting in here, with the door closed. But then, you know that perfectly well.'

Loyalty, of course, has to be earned over time. But you do have the right to ask for it at the outset – after that it's up to you to cherish it.

The chair of governors

The chair will come to you eagerly, full of ideas. This person, after all, has appointed you to the job and now expects wonders from you. In your first meeting, then, you must take charge of things. It needs to be clear that the chair is not your boss. Be polite and respectful, pointing out that you will welcome the chair into school at regular and agreed times. We say more about this in the section on relationships with the governing body.

The caretaker (site manager or whatever is the chosen title in your school)

Most caretakers are excellent, which is fortunate because there are times when he/she will have to go the extra mile to sort out a problem – perhaps one that threatens to close the school down. A good way to judge the caretaker's potential is to ask what are his/her problems. All caretakers have problems – they're endemic in a building used by hundreds of young people – but an astute one will know not to burden you with too many of them in that first meeting.

The senior admin person

The secretary may well be wondering just how much freedom of action they have. Make it clear that you expect them to run their department, but that as time goes on you'll go over all the office systems with them – finance, attendance, handling pupil data, ordering and receiving goods and services. The signal you're giving is that you'll let them get on with it, but that everything has to be done in accordance with proper financial procedures and with your own values, rules and priorities.

Get off on the right foot

Of all the people you have to manage and work with, these
four – deputy, chair, caretaker, secretary – are arguably the most
important. How can that be?, you ask. Surely the teachers are more
important?

That's not really the point. The simple fact is that there's
usually only one of each of these four people. Furthermore, each
of them controls a vital area where failure, or breakdown of trust,
has far-reaching consequences. If the caretaker drives home having
forgotten to report a fault with the boilers, you want him to
have the kind of commitment that will cause him to drive
straight back and put it right. You don't want him to say,
'Oh blow! They don't care about me, why should I care about
them?'

Each of these people, too, has relatively easy, frequent and regular
access to you. A class teacher, beavering away down the corridor, may
not speak to you for days – may not even want or need to. Your
secretary, though, will assuredly speak to you every day, as, probably,
will the caretaker and the deputy. And although you might not see your
chair of governors every day, it's fair to say that his/her phone calls are
usually put through or returned.

For all those reasons, it's important to get that first meeting right.
It's a matter of tone as well as content. You want to be friendly, but
you shouldn't get too close. As head you need to remember that you
may have to take any of your colleagues to task – perhaps even start
disciplinary proceedings. The closer you are to them, the more difficult
it will be.

A word about listening

Teachers aren't always natural listeners. They're too used to proclaiming.
Here are some thoughts about listening. The good leader is a listening
leader. And that means active listening, not just 'going-through-the-
motions' listening. Active listening means:

- giving full attention, signalled by being unhurried, by body language and by nods and encouraging words. 'Yes, I'm with you, go on. . . .'

- stopping the speaker and asking for clarification. A good way of doing this is to repeat the phrase and then simply ask for more detail. 'You say you have a group of children in your class who are easily distracted. I need to know about things like that. Say a little more about them will you. . . .'

- encouraging, and winkling out into the open, views that are different from your own. 'You look doubtful about that Jean. Come on, I need to hear what's on your mind. Nothing's off limits here.'

- following up – which may simply mean letting people know you haven't forgotten what they said. 'I've been thinking about that idea you had, Sam. Can you come and see me after school and just say a bit more about it?'

None of this is as easy as it sounds. We're teachers remember, and that means we're programmed to give information out rather than to take it in. Add to that the tendency for every new leader to want to get on with the job, and you have a recipe for riding heedlessly over the opinions of other people. Never forget that you are leading a team of knowledgeable professionals who have recent, direct experience of life at the sharp end of the institution you're now in charge of. The point about active listening is that it will get you to the nub of why people are doing what they're doing and thinking what they're thinking. You may well find that what seems like stubbornness, or simple failure to realise that there's a better way, is, in fact based on hard experience of what works and what doesn't in your particular neck of the woods.

Chapter 6
Where are you now? And where are you going?

Any discussion of planning for the future soon involves the words 'short', 'medium' and 'long'. So any school, and any leadership team, finds itself working towards those three sets of goals. Often they are set out in exactly that way on a document.

Beware

The trouble with that three-stage structure is that the short term tends to take over – as we've seen in our discussion of distractions in Chapter 2. Look at the children coming in on the first morning of your headship, and greeting you so expectantly, and there's no avoiding the fact that some of them – perhaps all of them – will have left before the vision you're carrying in your head has become reality. They want something to happen today.

That's fine, but you really can't afford to become so wrapped up in what's happening today that you don't have the time or the energy to engage with the future.

The answer is to realise that your short- and medium-term plans must actually arise out of the more strategic, long-term ones. So you simply cannot afford to ignore the long term. The fact is that if you find yourself identifying short-term goals first, and then working towards the more distant ones, you're actually running things from the wrong end.

▪ Good driving, proliferating plugs and rotten canoes

If you take an advanced driving course – the one that's used for Class 1 and Class 2 police drivers for example – you're taught always to look as far ahead as possible – beyond the next bend to where the tops of the telegraph poles show where the road goes after that, or to the brow of the hill beyond the one you're just coming to. Then you work back to the spot just ahead of your bonnet. Then you do it again, and again, automatically and more quickly than you can say it. That's because what you see in the distance affects your actions right now – the instructor actually uses the phrase, 'planning your driving'. But just like a head or a teacher, you also need to keep check on what's happening under your nose.

Here's an example more in tune with your decisions in school. Your ICT co-ordinator comes to say that the ICT room needs more electrical points. There are more computers, more printers. The case is open and shut so far as he/she's concerned.

But you know it isn't as simple as that – why?

Because:

▪ you don't know whether that room will always be the ICT room

▪ you don't know whether you're always even going to have a specialist ICT room, as ICT starts to embed itself in all aspects of school life.

But even so, maybe it'll be useful to have a room with lots of electrical points. . . . Decisions, decisions, decisions.

And that's just one dilemma out of many. Here's another one. A school in Birmingham had canoes rotting on the roof of an outbuilding. You don't need us to tell you why. They once had a teacher who was keen on taking children canoeing, and then he left. The school's priorities changed, and they couldn't just add 'ability to teach canoeing essential' to their job adverts.

We'd like to bet that more schools than you might think have, if not rotting canoes, then some equally redundant reminder of past enthusiasms lurking around the building or the grounds. Why not do an audit – mentally right now, or physically quite soon – and see if you can come up with some examples in your school. Each one isn't just a story in itself, but is a symbol of the perils of forward planning – of allowing an area of activity to develop around the only person who has the skill and enthusiasm to keep it going.

(While you're about it, why not put a staff bright spark on to the task of getting unused equipment back into action within the requirements of your current curriculum?)

It's not just a matter of sporty teachers who grow old or leave, or choir trainers who are replaced by orchestra enthusiasts. The rotten canoe syndrome is ubiquitous.

▦ You're my rock

Most schools – perhaps all schools – have a key member of staff, perhaps two or three, upon whom the head leans heavily. In a primary school it's probably a supremely able class teacher who is brilliant at motivating children and keeping them well behaved. So long as he/she's there, running the class that's most likely to give you headaches, everything is fine. 'I don't know what I'd do without you,' you say, if not out loud, then to yourself. Well, it's sensible forward planning to think the unthinkable. Try visualising one of your key people, and then thinking out what you would do if they were to disappear tomorrow. Even someone who looks settled for life can surprise you. Thirty-eight-year-olds get pregnant. Fifty-five-year-olds go off on VSO. Unlikely candidates get headships or open village shops. Don't be caught out, and certainly don't have, as your only plan, the aim of recruiting a straightforward replacement. It really doesn't happen like that. Consider the possibility that you may lose a brilliant teacher and be forced to replace him/her with a succession of supply teachers of varying quality. How would you manage that? Maybe you'll have to do a major reorganisation of class responsibilities. At least think about it. Like a Class One driver, look far ahead, then track back to what's happening now.

■ A planning strategy

One head, of a successful secondary school, tackles planning like this:

> 'We've set up what is in effect a virtual school. We call it (not its real name) "Garden Lane Academy 20 . . ." (a date that's always five years in the future). We try to envisage, with documents, diagrams, illustrations, what we want our school to be in five years time. We have a curriculum for it, a staffing pattern, a room allocation, even a skeleton timetable, a plan of the buildings. We don't let it roll towards us of course – we're continually pushing it forward so it's always five years away. The point then is that every decision we make is measured against a simple test – does it take us towards that school five years hence, or does it work against it? So – we have vacancy for a French teacher. But is French still on our future curriculum? How can we make sure we're not going into a cul-de-sac with this appointment?'

The distant view, you see, affects today's decisions.

Not everyone likes the 'virtual future school' idea – wrongly handled it can stifle creativity. Those Birmingham children, after all, did have a few glorious years of canoeing. Too much common sense might have deprived them of that. So in the end it's a matter of realising that long-term planning isn't a precise science, and the imprecision grows as we watch the accelerating rate with which ICT is making its presence felt. The greatest planning imperative, then, is flexibility. That means:

■ **flexibility in staffing** – You need multi-skilled and adaptable teachers and other staff who know that their jobs are changing faster than they can keep up. Try not to let people get set in their ways – always teaching in the same year group, always running the same sports and music groups. Train people for succession, stir things up a bit – but most importantly convince people that it's the right thing to do, and will be good for them personally as well as for the school. As part of this you need to be ready to make creative decisions about the deployment of part-time teachers, temporary teachers and teaching assistants.

- **flexibility of resources** – It's a bold head teacher who today invests large sums of money in textbooks. Already, as this book's being written, there are schools across the world where good computer software and hardware and the Internet have made textbooks entirely redundant. By the time you read this, you may well be saying, 'Tell me something new!'

- **flexibility in your admin staff** – Once, even big primaries had only one secretary. Some had none. Many even now don't have enough secretarial hours. And even if you can manage with one person, the traditional role has changed enormously, so you may need to share the work between two or more part-timers with different skills. Some new jobs have emerged, only partly driven by changes to what teachers are expected to do. So we have attendance officers, data managers, specialist receptionists, all carrying big responsibility and making it easier for teachers to concentrate on the core business of learning.

- **flexibility in the building** – It's another bold head teacher who agrees to a building project without considering what the school is going to be like in the future. What kind of spaces will you need? Will there even be what we now recognise as 'classes'? How many children will you have then? At the very least, it's not a good idea to make irrevocable decisions about changing the use of rooms.

Chapter 7
The legacy

You don't go into a vacuum. Your new school is a going concern. If you got run over by a bus on your way in on the first morning, the school would get through the day – and beyond, without much trouble. So you have to perform this very difficult trick of both fitting in and taking the reins. You have to be both passenger and chauffeur at the same time.

■ Following a saint

Taking over a failing school really is one of those classic, hand-rubbing, 'let's get stuck in' challenges. It's the sort of thing that a rising star who's on top of their game can relish. For one thing, it's often very clear to everyone that something has to be done – results down, misbehaviour up, parents voting with their feet. The aims, though probably not the means, are clear, and it's easy to get people to sign up to them.

What, though, about the less high-profile and, potentially, more difficult task of moving, as head, into a school that's at least on the face of it successful, following in the footsteps of a popular head who'd been there a long time.

A head says,

'He was a larger than life character. Parents, staff and children loved him. He'd created a school which was highly regarded in the community. Even when he took me on my first walk around the school you could see he had this genuine love for the place that was his baby.'

How do you follow that?

Essentially, of course, you don't. You come in as yourself and you manage in your own way. That's what you were recruited for. And you can be sure that no matter how revered was the previous head, different qualities are quickly recognised and loyalties transferred. (Think Truman after Roosevelt, Johnson after Kennedy.) The real professionals will make a determined effort to transfer their allegiance, and will deliberately not hark back to the earlier era. The ones who do cling to the past will quickly identify themselves as a disgruntled minority – and you get one of those in any sort of transition.

The complicating factor

Following a successful leader is one thing. The real challenge lies in convincing the staff that there are further improvements waiting to be made. And be assured that there always are. The truth is that the head who's leaving would usually be the first to acknowledge the need for more progress.

A retired head says,

> 'As I prepared to go, lots of people said they were sorry I was leaving, things wouldn't be the same – all the usual stuff. It struck me that my successor would be saddled with those nostalgic feelings about me and the way I did things. So I tried to make things a little easier by saying to everyone – staff, parents, governors – that one reason I was retiring just at this moment was because I knew there was a lot to be done – able children stretched, less able ones provided with more support, new government initiatives, new funding arrangements – and in my judgement someone else should come and take it all on, with renewed energy. I don't know whether people got the message – some did, some didn't, I suppose. But at least I was clearly on the record as saying that there was work to do.'

The most difficult scenario, probably, is where the need for improvement is real but difficult to spot. Here's another head.

*'The problem was simple really. Results were going up – not a lot,
but the direction was right. The trouble was, the value-added score
was going down. That's not uncommon these days. The reason was
that children were coming in from the two feeder infant schools
with higher and higher scores, year on year. We were improving at
Year Six, but the improvement at the incoming end was faster. So
value-added score was squeezed. Most staff could see that, but some
found it difficult to take. They'd say things like, "We're working hard,
driving up our test scores in Year Six. I don't know what else we can
do". Or else they'd cast doubt on the Key Stage 1 results. "Do we
know they're as accurate as they should be?" '*

(That's happening more and more in schools that take children from
an earlier stage – junior schools taking children from the infants,
secondaries taking children from primary. A drive for improvement in a
'feeder' school, perhaps under a new head, or with local authority
support, can take the school next in line by surprise, especially if there's
been some complacency. Ofsted, right from the start, has been critical
of 'cruising' schools, which, often, are the ones caught out by subtle
changes in the value-added data. It's worth mentioning too, while we're
about it, that the reverse case is also increasingly common – a school
with apparently poor Year Six results is actually increasing its
value-added score.)

So here you see what's probably the most difficult of all starts to a
new head's career – walking into a school that's orderly, hard-working,
well thought of and, crucially, with improving results, and announcing
that performance isn't good enough.

How do you handle that?

The head says,

*'I got other people to support me. I had a consultant in to go over the
performance data with the staff – an expert in interpreting and
explaining pupil-performance figures. She didn't say anything
different from what I'd been saying, but she was an outsider – not
even from the local authority. Gradually, between us, we convinced
the key people that the story told by the decline in value-added was a
real one – that it had to be checked and that it was no good looking*

*suspiciously at the KS1 data in the hope of finding some sort of
explanation there.'*

This head also set out to sell staff the idea that this was a
whole-school issue.

*'I knew that the Key Stage 2 results weren't just an issue for Year Six.
It was necessary to look at teaching and learning all the way through.'*

▪ Traditions

Every new head will tell you that right from the start, and even before
that, people who know and love the school – staff, parents, governors,
children – will come up and ask you anxiously whether you are going to
continue with some of the events and happenings that are seen as part
of the school. Maybe your predecessor ran a wonderful annual concert.
If that's so, then you can bet you'll have a succession of people saying,
'Will we still be having the big concert?'

Be assured this is no small thing. There are schools where families
have chosen to send their children there on the strength of something
like that, and where children look forward all the way through the
infants to the time when they can be in the play, the band, the choir,
the team or whatever it is that's made the school famous in the locality.

It's not easy to face up to this. As a new head you have a host of
priorities – and it's very likely that maintaining and improving the
quality of teaching and learning, and the results that follow, is at the top
of the list. It's at least possible, too, that you lack the particular skills
that have made the big concert, the super choir or the brass band your
predecessor's pride and joy.

In the last resort, you are going to navigate this particular problem
alone, guided by, and trusting in, the professional and leadership skills
that got you the job. It's a balancing act, and here to help you are some
of the factors that you have to weigh on either side.

1 First and last, you're the boss. And in those early days, people want
you to succeed. If you're clear about your priorities, and they are

obvious and intelligible to everyone, you'll be surprised at how readily people will accept whatever you decide.

2   Some traditions are certainly worth keeping. The school belongs to its community, and you need to take their feelings into account.

3   A school that has no hinterland of teams, activities, music, dance, is impoverished in a way that will impinge on the very priorities you deem so important.

4   If your predecessor had his/her own 'baby' – a choir, a band, a team – then it's possible that someone else could have been doing it but was held back.

5   Similarly, there may be a member of staff who's been longing to start something else, but because of your predecessor's 'big thing' didn't have the elbow room.

6   Schools are evolutionary – there's an ebb and flow of strengths and specialisms as people come and go. Be conscious of that, and go with the incoming tide.

7   It's very possible that your colleagues are quietly ready for a change and will be relieved to be freed from the treadmill of a massive annual event.

8   If you do bite the bullet and drop a much loved tradition, more people than you would have imagined will go with you, and for the rest – well, the dust will settle more quickly than you might think.

Chapter 8

Resistance to change

There are always resisters to change and innovation – people who dislike a new policy and work to undermine it, or who can't come to terms with ICT or with a change of class or subject. The secret of dealing with them is not to spend too much time in face-to-face persuasion. What you do is work with the people who want to go with you, to build a structure that irresistibly enfolds the others and draws them in. It may be, for example, that you'll build a communications system based on the school network, so that any ICT resister begins to find themselves shut out of what's happening. Yet even that may well leave a few hard cases untouched, in which case you may have to work around them until such time as you can find a way of winkling them out.

All of that depends, of course, on winning over from the start enough people to create a critical mass of support. Get it wrong and you'll have the opposite – a critical mass of resistance.

Here's a true story.

A keen young male deputy head – let's call him Steve, which isn't his name – became head of a large primary school. It was obvious from the questions he was asked at interview that the governors were looking for someone with new ideas who would bring improved results and better behaviour. In fact after he'd been offered the job, and accepted it, the chair of governors took Steve on one side and told him in no uncertain terms that they expected him 'to shake things up a bit'.

Much later in his career – when he was well into his second headship in fact – Steve looked back on that conversation.

'At that point it was about the worst thing that could have happened to me,' he said. 'Because I took it as a licence to go in bull headed, throwing my weight about. I didn't know any better you see. As a deputy I had great respect for my head teacher – fear almost – and I assumed that I would be able to command the same sort of feelings among the people I was now being asked to lead.'

One of the things that Steve had noticed about his new school, during his initial look around and then later when he visited, was that there was a distinct lack of written policies.

'I couldn't understand how they'd got away with it,' he said. 'Then I realised that in fact they'd been lucky to escape inspection – it was in the quite early days of Ofsted. Obviously, though, Ofsted were going to arrive before long, probably when I was still a relative newcomer, and they'd be down on me like a ton of bricks if I hadn't done something about introducing some written policies.'

During the summer holiday before he took up his new post in September, Steve thought a great deal about this. He decided to make a start on putting things right by writing one of the main policies himself.

'I decided to target behaviour', he recalled. 'It was pretty clear to me that behaviour was a problem in the school. The chair of governors had told me so, and in any case I'd seen enough on my visits to know that things weren't right – too much unruly behaviour in the corridors, noisy classes, teachers shouting and so on.'

The school that Steve came from had what he considered a really good behaviour policy based on a closely defined system of rewards and sanctions, so Steve wrote out a version of it aimed at his new school.

'It was quite a long document', he said. 'Outlining the way that rewards and sanctions should be used – merit marks, names written on the blackboard, referrals to the head, letters home and so on. I word processed it all up, did about 20 copies, put them all into nice folders with the school name and crest on the front and then, just before the new term started in September, I took them into school and went round putting them on the teachers' desks.'

At the first staff meeting, on the day before term started, Steve introduced himself to the staff.

'Then after the usual polite introductions', he said, 'I told them I was sure they'd agree with me that behaviour in the school just wasn't good enough, and that in order to tackle it I wanted them to follow a new behaviour policy. I pointed out that they all had a copy of it on their desks, and that I wanted them to study it and get it into action in their classrooms and across the school as quickly as possible.'

When Steve was telling this story – as an older and considerably wiser head teacher – he paused at this point and smiled. Then he went on,

'Looking back', he said, 'I can hardly believe what I did. Oh, there was nothing wrong with the new behaviour policy. In fact we eventually did get something like it up and running. Because, you see, there was no doubt at all that a new approach was needed. Most of the staff realised that very well. What I didn't realise in my enthusiasm and callow youth was that you just can't go into a new place, staffed by experienced people, and start telling everyone what to do. Especially when it comes to something as sensitive as the way they deal with the behaviour of their own pupils.'

The reaction of the staff to Steve's policy was universally hostile. The deputy head – who hadn't been consulted, remember – came in at the end of the first day, closed the door, and told Steve very frankly that his behaviour policy document had turned into a time bomb.

'She pointed out to me', said Steve, 'That I was a newcomer. She said that I had to win respect, and couldn't impose it. She said that she'd read my behaviour policy and it seemed fine, but that all her colleagues were going through it with a fine toothcomb finding the holes in it and talking up its faults among themselves.'

◼ A new broom

Steve, in a way, was a victim of the myth which is enshrined in the old saying, 'A new broom sweeps clean'.

Now it's obvious that being a new head brings some opportunities to make changes – to that extent the old saying is true. What's entirely false, though, is the idea that being new – being a new broom – provides a chance to ride roughshod over existing ways of doing things, without regard for the opinions and feelings of the people who have been working there for years.

Steve faced serious resistance to his new policy in the form of constant questioning about it and nit-picking in meetings.

'People were constantly coming up with "what ifs" ', said Steve. ' "What if this won't work, or that? What do we do if so and so. . . .?" All those obstructive questions that betray people's underlying resistance to change.'

Chapter 9
Monitoring

You have many responsibilities, but one of the most onerous is that of monitoring teaching and learning in the school. You must, therefore, give serious consideration, and time, right from the start of your headship – and before if the opportunity's there – to deciding how you're going to do it.

How to start?

■ The quick overview

- ■ Read any performance data that's available – from Ofsted, the local authority and held within the school.

- ■ Visit classrooms – not, in the first instance, for formal observation, but as a visitor to greet children and teachers.

- ■ Be around on the playground and in the corridors observing how children and adults act towards each other.

- ■ Go to the school gate and talk to parents and reassure them that you're ready to listen if they need to come and see you.

- ■ Judge for yourself the strengths and weaknesses of individual teachers. (Whether you read any files on this compiled by your predecessor is up to you. There's something to be said for not doing it, though. You do need to make up your mind in an unprejudiced way– and it'll help your relationship with colleagues if they know they're not being prejudged.)

A head says,

> 'You're told things by the local authority and the previous head. I was told who my failing teachers were, who my good teachers were, who'd had problems, who'd had special coaching. When I went in and observed, and found out that what they'd told me was accurate I actually felt better. I realised it wasn't just me having these opinions.'

Then you move into a routine of continuous monitoring of what's happening in the school, using these techniques.

▧ Observing lessons

There's no shortage of guidance about observing lessons. The Ofsted criteria, as set down in the Inspection handbook, make a mutually understood and objective starting point. But remember the points below.

1   Set up a properly organised programme of observation, so that people know when they're going to be observed, and can be properly briefed in advance and debriefed afterwards. Don't do things at the last minute which, in effect, makes a colleague the victim of your own lack of organisation. 'Sorry to dump this on you, Jack, but as I have half an hour to spare, I'm coming into the next lesson.'

2   You're not the only person observing others. In many schools everyone observes everyone else. Your job is to manage this so that your supportive values are clear throughout. That means you'll need to observe the observers at times, and check on the way the follow-up discussions are handled.

3   If you do need to do a short-notice observation – perhaps to help a colleague who's preparing for a course or an interview – you can still agree enough notice to keep any sense of urgency at bay.

4   Although you may be using inspection criteria, you're not just an inspector, but a supportive colleague, so your approach should be positive.

5   Remember that the emphasis is on teaching and learning. So you need to know what the children are supposed to be learning, and whether that's being achieved.

6   Don't measure the teacher against yourself. You aren't leading a team of clones.

7   Above all, don't use a 'scattergun' approach. Agree the focus of our observation, and concentrate on that in your follow-up discussion.

A head teacher says,

> 'One thing that can happen is that a person mentoring an NQT can become quite defensive. Because of the mentor's nurturing role they may find it difficult to accept that things are not as they should be, and frankly that's quite hard to handle. In the end you may need an opinion from someone else – an authority adviser or inspector, for example.'

▨ Looking at the books

Don't forget to check children's work, making comparisons within and across classes. Heads who do this regularly will tell you that it's a very clear way of seeing whether or not there's proper evidence of progression and differentiation. Differences between classes in the year group show up quite starkly, as do the cases where a child or a group hasn't progressed well in the next year group.

A head says,

> 'That one (children who fall back when they move to the next year group) is tricky. It needs careful handling. Teachers are very possessive of their classes and very ready sometimes to say, "They weren't like that with me!". But the story isn't always as straightforward as it

seems. I know because it happened to me when I was a class teacher. My class one year had been with another teacher where they'd been under the thumb. When they came to me I wanted them to be independent learners, finding their own equipment and so on, and they found it hard. It took them a while to get used to it. And so their work seemed to take a dip. What I've learned from that is that when you do see something like this in children's work, you go into the class and find out what's happening before you make quick judgements.'

This can work between schools as well as between classes. Another head, of a junior school, says,

'The new head of the infants came to see me. She wanted me to know that she was reorganising the school in such a way that the first cohorts of children coming to me might not have reached the same levels of attainment. She felt she wanted to make sure that firm foundations of understanding and love of learning were put in place, and this might be at the expense of test results. It was a courageous decision, but an honourable one that was actually an example to all of us.'

■ Problems with monitoring

It's one thing to talk about establishing a predictable monitoring routine, but maintaining it in the real world of school is something else. Not only do you have a whole range of other demands on your time, but teachers can be absent from school. The only thing to be said about this is that the observation of classroom work ought to be high on your priority list. Maintaining the quality of teaching and learning in your classrooms is what you're actually there for.

Do you cancel a teacher's observation because he/she says they're not well, or has not long returned from an illness? The answer is that Ofsted wouldn't cancel. Their line is that if the teacher's in school, the children are entitled to their full attention, and by and large your approach should be the same. But you're not Ofsted, and as you get to know your people there may be some exceptions to this. It's not easy to think of any though, and very few really conscientious teachers would expect any concessions.

Supply staff

The other question that arises from staff absence is about the observation of supply teachers. Do you observe a supply teacher? Clearly you need to know what their performance is like – for your sake, for the sake of the children and for the sake of others who may employ the person.

If the teacher is only in for a day, it's clearly impossible to give them proper notice of a formal observation. It's not difficult to get an impression, though, from colleagues, from breaktime chats, from the way the children behave and, importantly, from the work that's been done during the day. Don't just put the teacher in the room and forget about them. You may want to employ them again, perhaps for a longer period, or they may become a candidate for a permanent job, so arm yourself with as much knowledge as you can.

Children's opinions

Never forget the voice of the children. A head says,

> '*I choose them totally at random and sit them round the table. Sometimes I just grab a child in the corridor. They'll be frank about their likes and dislikes, and they have very firm opinions. They can tell you whether a lesson is good or not, and they can describe their teachers' little traits. They're more astute than you think sometimes.*'

Parents' opinions

Talk informally to parents all the time – at the gate, while they're waiting for children. Consider using a questionnaire that mirrors the one used by Ofsted.

Chapter 10
Supporting and developing staff

A head says,

> 'One of my strongest memories is of being at a meeting at which one of the speakers was a senior business leader who happened to be a school governor. He said that he was constantly surprised and disappointed to find that schools weren't very good at – this is the phrase he used – "bringing their people on". To me, the phrase itself was interesting, because its very casualness indicates a mindset where it's quite normal to think in terms of developing staff, just part of working life. So far as he was concerned, he explained later, you constantly looked at colleagues in terms of what they were going to be doing next. It was a continuous process, not something that just came to life occasionally.'

Well, are we good at 'bringing our people on'? Better, perhaps than we were when that businessman spoke. Better now there's a National College for School Leadership, and a set of development structures – performance management, a ladder of qualifications from NQT to LPSH, all of which the aspirant or serving head has to know about.

It's still important, though, to have the mindset – the attitude, and the systems, that help people to think in terms of continuing professional development.

What this means is trying hard to uncover people's strengths and release them to everyone's benefit. One person who has tried hard to find a way of doing this is Dame Sheila Wallis who, when she was Head of Davison High School in Worthing, developed what she called 'The Expert Trail'. What it does is provide a structure that defines, recognises and celebrates levels of personal achievement in an area of professional study that the member of staff has chosen. Ideally – and it worked like this at Davison – every single member of staff, teaching and support, was on the Trail, pursuing a chosen area of professional development. It went in stages, and, crucially, there was extra money for people as they progressed up the ladder – not a lot, but it's the recognition that counts.

In recent years, the Expert Trail has taken root in a number of places around the country, particularly in primary schools. And it's allowing people to develop in some interesting ways. In one primary, for example, a teaching assistant who was capable in the classroom but shy outside of it decided to become an expert in a particular system of helping children with early numeracy. She studied it, and applied it in her work, to the point where she became someone who spoke on teachers' courses and was a consultant to the system's developers.

Individual stories and systems, though, aren't the point. What matters is that you can be sure every one of your teachers and support staff would really like to develop further an aspect of their professionalism – differentiation, perhaps, or emotional development, or behaviour management, or sign language, or approaches to dyslexia – there's really no end to the possibilities. It's really not beyond the wit of any head to agree with each colleague on a focus for development that suits both the person and the school.

What happens then, of course, is that you're faced with how to make use of the newfound expertise. All that needs to be said about that is if you can't find an effective outlet, in your school, for someone who's become knowledgeable about dyslexia, signing, differentiation or numeracy, then you're the one who needs the mindset adjustment.

■ Coming up on the rails

In this regard, you really must take notice of the huge changes afoot in the world of support staff. It's not unusual now for any school to have more support staff than teachers. Their work has changed dramatically. They're having more training, and taking more responsibility. We have higher level teaching assistants, cover supervisors, and a whole career ladder is opening up for technicians in science and in design technology. Don't be caught out by this. Your support staff, properly deployed and recognised, can be a real force for improvement in your school. Learn about their work, listen to them, find out about training possibilities and look after their pay and working conditions. One of the big grumbles in any school centres around support staff who feel that they're marginalised and that their skills aren't recognised. There are still schools where they aren't invited into the staffroom. How long will it take you to put that right?

A senior science technician says,

> *'I tell my technicians that every so often they should remove their white coats and walk around looking like everyone else. It's surprising how many people suddenly notice them for the first time, and start acting normally towards them.'*

She may have been exaggerating, but I doubt it, and in any case you can see the point.

■ Staff development – key points

Look at each member of staff through a special pair of glasses with, 'Where is this person going next?' engraved on them.

Talk to your colleagues with those glasses on.

Encourage colleagues to think beyond the track they're currently on – to look at other subjects, other areas of teaching and responsibility and qualification. Ask, 'What have you really always wanted to do?' But also aim to get people saying, 'You know, I never thought of that!'

Support their interests and ambitions. If money's needed, don't give up, scratch around, look for sources of funding, develop a nose for it.

Know their expertise. Be interested in it. Then use it. You get angry when when a shopkeeper or bartender says, 'There isn't much call for that, sir,' so please don't be guilty of saying it yourself.

Try a wide range of colleagues – and not only teachers — as trainers in twilight sessions. If necessary, say, 'Don't worry. I'll be there with you'. You'll all make discoveries about each other.

Pay particular attention to colleagues who are just beyond their NQT year. If they're going to stay the course they may need picking up and nurturing till they get to the point where they're ready for big responsibility. Find projects they can lead, people they can mentor, working groups they can chair.

Chapter 11

ICT

Within a few years – and maybe much sooner than any of us think, our schools are going to be transformed by a quantum leap in their use of ICT. The key will lie in a deeper understanding of computer-held, pupil-assessment data and increasing use of learning platforms, which, properly used, will change the whole nature of schooling. Hannah Jones, Director of Strategic Leadership of ICT at the National College for School Leadership said in an interview with the author at the end of 2006,

> *Children learn with ICT when they become creators and not consumers – creating content, developing peer-to-peer relationships. A head teacher will have a thousand experts in the school, and the task is to harness their knowledge – teams of pupils working alongside teams of staff. It needs to be approached from the learner's point of view, with the teacher as facilitator.*

Any head being appointed now needs to be aware of the possibilities of learning platforms, and the challenges for the way their school works in the years to come.

That's a tall order, and before you can even think about it, you need to be up to speed with what you already have, and that means understanding the potential of your management information system.

We've already discussed the importance to the head teacher of data. It's data that provides the information about what's happening, without which it's hardly possible to run the school.

Where, though, does the data come from? Obviously, in the first
instance it comes from the classroom, as assessments of pupil
performance, attendance and behaviour. It sits in pupils' books
(as marks and comments), in attendance registers, in teachers' mark
books (paper or electronic), on exam and test papers. So long as the
data is in that form, it's difficult for you, as head teacher, to make real
sense of it. You can try, of course, as your predecessors have over the
years, by sampling it – looking through selected pupils' books, taking
in mark books, setting up a system of summary sheets, discussing
progress with teachers, parents and the pupils themselves. All are worth
doing – and continuing – in some form even when more sophisticated
data handling systems are in place.

Clearly, though, what we're leading up to here is the way that the
handling and analysis of pupil data has been revolutionised over the
past 15 or 20 years by the advent of computer software in general and
the specialised school management information system (MIS) in
particular.

It's hardly possible to overestimate the importance of the modern
MIS and its potential as a tool for school improvement. Awareness of
this among heads, though, has been slow to catch up. It's not difficult to
see why. MIS had its origins, in the late eighties, in the need for schools
to look after their own finances. It became associated, as a result, with
finance, the school secretary and the school office. Now, even though
MIS has expanded enormously and is now capable of handling,
analysing and presenting useful data on how well – or badly – the
school, or an individual pupil, is doing, it still finds it difficult to shake
off that 'school office' association.

In 2006 a major MIS supplier surveyed a large number of local
authority support teams, who reported to them that only a quarter of
schools were using their MIS packages to the full. These support teams
then went on to estimate how many head teachers were fully confident
in using their MIS for school improvement. Somewhere between 0 and
5 per cent was the answer. Both figures were for all schools. Primaries, it
was said, came out worse than secondaries.

The lesson here is that every head, or aspiring head, needs to
understand the potential of their school's MIS. That doesn't mean being
conversant with the technicalities. It doesn't even mean knowing how to

dodge around all of the myriad screens, modules and sections. What it does mean, at the most basic level, is knowing that the MIS can supply valuable data about what's happening in the school. It can give you the means to, among other things:

- track attendance progress over time, across year groups and classes and at the level of individual pupils

- track pupil progress – individuals, classes, year groups, the whole school – making whatever comparisons you need

- provide performance data appropriate for a range of users – school management, class teachers, parents, governors, the pupils themselves (who can become fully involved in their own target setting).

This isn't a handbook on how to use MIS for school improvement. The message for now is that you need to know what your MIS will do for you. To make the most of it, work with your authority support team and/or the system's suppliers. Don't switch off, or make the mistake of thinking, or saying, 'Oh computers! That's for someone else to worry about.' The drive has to come from the head.

How to proceed

1   You already have a management information system sitting on your school network. (Capita's 'Sims' is the most common system, but it's far from being the only one. There are about six main suppliers.) It's already being used to transmit statutory data to the authority and the government. Now you need to make sure that it's working just as hard for you.

2   Ask the question 'How can I use the data in my MIS to improve teaching and learning in our school?' Ask it of your authority MIS support team, and also of the supplier of the MIS system. You need to spend some time on this, but it will pay off in the end.

3   From your supplier and the support team, glean examples of schools that are further down the road with management ICT than you are. Visit them, with key members of staff.

4   As you become more confident in your use of the MIS, begin to involve your colleagues. The MIS needs to be available to them, on the network. For this, they need enough hardware – readily available desktop and laptop computers. Do the budget sums for this.

5   Remember two key principles. One is that it's teachers who make the difference. The information provided by the MIS helps in decision-making, but it doesn't bring about improvement on its own. The second is that the data coming out of the MIS is only as good as what's fed into it. There's no point arguing about a difference of two percentage points in a child's assessment scores if you can't be sure that the scores are the result of accurate observation or testing.

Chapter 12

To teach or not to teach?

Should a primary head teach for at least part of the time? We all know that there's no simple answer. Many heads, for example, have no choice. In a very small school the head's going to be virtually a full-time class teacher, and for some way up the scale of school sizes, staffing levels are set on the assumption that the head is going to be part of the teaching team.

No, the question has to be asked differently. In fact there are really probably three questions.

1   Should the head teach for more time than the staffing position actually demands?

2   Assuming that the head has to do some teaching, should he/she have a fixed and regular timetable?

3   Should the head be the first call when it comes to covering for staff absence?

Before we even attempt to answer any or all of these questions, let's hear this story from a head teacher who's recently retired.

> *'For several years I taught a half timetable – I actually shared a class with a part-time teacher. That was in a school which was theoretically big enough for the head to be entirely non-teaching. Why did I do it? Because the numbers in the year groups were awkward and the governors were determined to avoid mixed-age grouping. As a*

*result we had some very small classes. That made us, in practice,
under staffed and I had to teach to make up the numbers.'*

So was this head doing more teaching than the staffing position
demanded? Well, yes. The local authority believed that the school had
enough staff for the head not to teach. They felt very strongly that the
governors were being unreasonable in sticking out for single-age
grouping when many schools successfully run mixed-age classes.

The authority also felt that a head with such a heavy teaching load
couldn't effectively monitor teaching and learning across the school.
Ofsted felt the same, and said so in an inspection report.

The plus point – and it was valued by everyone – lay in the small
classes. Research may cast doubt on the importance of class size, but
anyone who's taught a class of 22 children certainly appreciates it.

The problem solved itself eventually when the head retired early with
ill health. The deputy head took over, initially on an acting basis, later
permanently. He felt less able to withstand the authority's arguments,
and so he and the governors reluctantly agreed that they should go to
mixed-age grouping.

■ Why do heads teach?

- ■ The head in our story was at least partly driven to teach a
  significant timetable by the fact that she was extremely good at it.
  So that's one reason why heads teach – they genuinely feel that
  children shouldn't be deprived of their classroom skills.

- ■ Another reason is that they feel they should be demonstrating their
  ability to do the front line job.

- ■ And then, of course, there's simple escapism – the head's desire to
  get out of the office, away from the phone and into contact with
  the simple and stark realities of the classroom.

None of these reasons are bad ones. It's just a matter of being honest
with yourself and lining up your own personal reasons against the needs
of the school.

Chapter 13
Money

'Money', said one head we talked to about this book, 'is dangerous stuff. It can rear up and bite you.'

The reasoning behind this rather alarming assessment isn't difficult to find. It lies in the following contrast.

On the one hand, there's a head teacher who's come up through the classroom, an excellent professional, eager to concentrate on teaching and learning in the school. Other aspects of the job, including looking after the school's finances are seen as irksome and intrusive.

'If I'd wanted to look after money I'd have become a bank manager', says this head.

On the other hand, there's thousands, perhaps millions of pounds of public money, extracted from reluctant tax and council tax payers. These unwilling benefactors' elected representatives are duty bound to ensure that every penny is wisely used and accounted for and they've put in place a coldly efficient finance department to make sure that it happens.

As a result, it's fatally easy for a school's accounts to get into a muddle, and it's very common for a new head to discover that things are not as they should be. There may be invoices that have been overlooked and which make the budget look less healthy than anyone thought. Or it may be that there's slackness in the way that cash is handled, or that the procedure for ordering and receiving goods isn't strictly according to the book. In most authorities a school where the head is leaving is supposed to be visited by the internal audit department, but this doesn't always happen.

So, even though it's not your mainstream interest, this is what you have to do as early as possible in your headship.

1   Go through the local authority's financial procedures manual. If you can't find it, get hold of your own copy as soon as possible. Study it carefully, with your school and its people in mind.

2   With the regulations in mind – and in your hand – go through the way your school office deals with finance. Pay particular attention to the way cash is handled and accounted for – dinner money, school trip money, photograph money, petty cash.

3   Check the way that goods and services are ordered, received and paid for. Don't forget the caretaker's materials in this. Make sure the correct procedures are followed.

4   Now be prepared to stand your ground and insist that things are done properly. This might be difficult, and there may be resentment – 'We've done it like this for years and I have to say nobody has questioned it before . . .'. But remember that if things go badly wrong, you will be in the firing line.

5   As an added precaution, talk to internal audit about the procedures in your school. If necessary ask them to come in and do a full audit.

6   As an added incentive, remember that the following things have all happened in schools known to the authors.

■   An incoming head discovered that the secretary had been stealing from the children's dinner money for years. The benign and other-worldly chair of governors refused to believe it even in the face of the evidence until the heavies were called in from internal audit.

■   Another incoming head – and this is very common – found that a secretary, despairing of the school's general decline into chaos under a head who was in depression, had more or less given up and stuffed unpaid invoices into drawers.

■   And yet another incoming head found that his predecessor had been in the habit of giving the leader of the annual residential trip a large sum of cash to pay for 'sundries' and failing to have it accounted for. The new head's insistence on tightening this up caused the trip leader to withdraw from the job in a huff.

■ And there was the head who discovered that her predecessor had more or less furnished her house from educational supply catalogues. She apparently felt that, after years of service, it was somehow her due. She was lucky to escape prison.

■ Two teachers, given free rein to handle, over more than a year, money being saved by children for a skiing trip, privately bought shares with it, thinking to make a killing. You can guess the rest.

■ School fund

So far in this chapter we've been thinking mainly of public funds – the money delegated to the school budget by the local authority for its core purposes. Usually, though, it's not the only money that the school handles. There are often unofficial or 'voluntary' funds. So, for example, there may be a school fund that's fed from jumble sales, summer fairs and so on. Or there may be a charity fund that's quietly used to help needy children with uniform or school trips. The Parent Teacher Association (PTA) may have a fund, and there may be money coming in from families saving towards a school trip. All such funds are off the official authority balance sheet. Nevertheless – for that very reason indeed – they have to be carefully administered, for the head is directly responsible for them to the governors. Again, the financial procedures manual will give essential guidance, for this is another area where slackness may have crept in. Everyone will know, for example, that cheques drawn on school fund need two signatures – one normally being that of the head, the other perhaps of another member of staff, or of a parent. It's a sensible safeguard, but it's amazing how often the head is asked to sign a bundle of blank cheques just to expedite, for example, the arrangements for the summer fair. It's often done so casually – 'Could you just sign a few cheques please?' – that it seems churlish to refuse. But refuse you must, and put up bravely with any huffing and puffing that follows.

Having made sure that school funds are properly run, you should then check what the arrangements are for having them audited. Sometimes there's slackness here too. Some authorities require only that they be audited by someone unconnected with the organisation. Better, on the whole, have them audited by a qualified accountant. The job will then be done properly and also be seen to be done properly, which is equally important.

PTA funds

The PTA, the Parents' Association or the 'Friends of the School', whatever it's name, isn't part of the school. If it's properly constituted it will be a separate charity. It's in your interest, though, to see that it's properly run, so you and the governors can do no better than refer the people running your PTA to the National Confederation of Parent Teacher Associations www.ncpta.org.uk who can provide all the necessary advice, including a model constitution.

The budget process

It's not our purpose here to take you through the details of setting and monitoring the school budget. If you're a local authority school there's plenty of guidance on this. What we can do, though, is urge the new or aspiring head to take notice of some principles.

- Talk to other heads of schools like yours about how they set and manage their budgets.

- Ask other heads about the quality of support and advice that's available from the authority. If it's good – and it usually is – don't stint on taking it, even if it costs money. In many cases, a finance officer will come into school regularly and take much of the burden from you. Unless you have particular skills in this area, do accept all the help you can get.

■ Remember the key principle which is that the school improvement plan and the budget go hand in hand. All that you plan for in the school has to be paid for, and you have to recognise and show this.

■ Don't simply carry the budget forward year to year adding a bit here, taking away a bit there. Question all the headings and relate them to your plans for the school.

■ Involve governors at every stage – the whole thing's their responsibility, and in some cases they'll have the skills and the enthusiasm to give you real support.

■ Two cautionary tales from a head

'One of our parents ran an excellent small carpentry and general joinery business. He wanted to know if there was a possibility of work around the school. I knew there was a system of approved suppliers to the authority, and so I recommended that he be placed on it. The authority took a look at him, and agreed that he could be approved. He was very grateful. Then at some later stage, while he was working in the school, I asked him if he'd take a look at a job in my house. I told him I expected to be invoiced and to pay the proper rate. My main motive in asking him was that I knew he'd do a good job. In the end, though, when he'd finished the job in my house, he flatly refused to take any payment. Even though I explained to him that it was important for me to pay, he dug his heels in, and ended up walking away, waving away my protests. This deeply embarrassed me, and I learned a lesson about how easily corruption can creep into any system.'

And the other story?

'Very early in my headship I realised we needed another overhead projector. Without thinking I phoned a discount photographic store *in town and got one at what I thought was a good price. When the invoice went to county they looked at it and got on the phone to inform me that I could have got the same OHP from county supplies for half the price. Part of the problem, I realised, was that I'd been too busy in my first term to attend a meeting for new heads at which such things were explained. Another lesson.'*

Some you win, some you lose. All you can do is try hard not to get into significant trouble.

Chapter 14
Relationships with parents

We hear a great deal about difficulties with parents, and there's no doubt that long-serving heads have seen significant change in the home–school axis. Parents, on the whole, are less ready to accept everything that school says – not just on the traditional issues of uniform, hairstyle, jewellery and the like, but on more central, curricular areas such as special educational needs.

In many ways that's inevitable and good. For years we've paid lip service in schools to 'partnership' and we can't complain when it's interpreted as a true, two-way relationship.

One by-product, though, aggravated by a general increase in litigiousness in society has been a greater number of confrontational incidents. At one level there have been invasions of classrooms by irate parents and actual assaults; at another level, lawsuits brought against schools and authorities. What's to be done?

■ Building trust

The long-term aim is to build a foundation of trust against which confrontational incidents become rare and atypical. An important part of this process is to ensure that parents don't get unpleasant surprises about their children's performance or behaviour. Parents shouldn't, for example, open a report expecting a row of 'As' only to find 'Ds' instead. That means establishing a line of constant contact, keeping families in touch with their children's progress, calling them in where necessary.

You'll need to keep on top of this, because a child's performance can change significantly but gradually over half a term or more. Systems in school should be able to track this, and the people in immediate charge of the child's progress – whether class teacher, year leader, subject leader, assessment co-ordinator – be pursuing the reasons. It's very easy, though, for parents to be left out of the loop, and you need to put in the policies and practices that ensure this doesn't happen. The last thing you want to hear from a parent is, 'Why didn't someone tell us what was going on?'

■ Providing the evidence

Evidence goes a long way to promoting agreement and nipping confrontation in the bud. When you meet a parent, whether at a formal parents' meeting or for a one-off interview, make sure you can back up your statements with evidence.

So if you say, 'We're concerned about her behaviour,' you must go on to give chapter and verse about actual incidents, dated and recorded.

Similarly, if it's a matter of declining performance, you should have samples of work, with test and assessment data, showing the trend.

And you should be on to this sort of thing soon enough to avoid the accusation, 'You should have told us earlier'.

It's a fine balance, of course – you want to keep parents in the picture, but you don't want to be accused of fussing about minor changes in the overall picture. There's no easy answer to that dilemma except to say that it's a matter of knowing your children and their families and trusting your teachers. In other words, it's about using the professional judgement that's got you where you are.

■ Winning support

Parents want, and deserve, more than just information about a child's declining performance. They want to know what you're going to do about it, and what they can do to help.

Again, you need to be ready with specifics – a different maths group, an 'on-report' system, a booster class – all of that's down to you and your team, but be ready with it. A great deal of parental grumbling is caused by a feeling that the school is being vague – 'pussy footing', 'wishy washy'. What they often mean is that the school's explained the problem but not come up with any solutions. So be positive, decisive, precise and clear.

That's the point at which you ask the parents how they think they might be able to help, which is a better way into the discussion than setting down a list of requirements. Often the parental response will be much more draconian than you either expect or want. 'Right! He's grounded for the rest of the year, and he can say goodbye to his Playstation. . . .'

If that's what you hear, this is the moment for you to be conciliatory and make the point that you're accepting the main responsibility for putting things right, and that what you need from them is interest and encouragement – to look in the homework diary, give space and time for school work and activities, all those things that you take for granted but that many parents will appreciate seeing spelled out and explained.

When it goes pear-shaped

You'll have the occasional visit from an irate parent. Everybody does. A head says,

> 'In the very early days of my headship it was my turn to host the local heads' meeting straight after school. I was so proud and eager to please. I did all the usual things – entrance hall primped and polished, library looking wonderful, tea and cakes nicely laid out. When there were about a dozen of us gathered, making small talk, the next one came in saying, "Irate parent down there!"
>
> I thought she was winding me up, but sure enough there was a very aggressive, very angry man in the entrance hall shouting the odds and demanding my presence. I was ashamed –

surely my colleagues would think I couldn't keep things under
control? But of course they'd all, every single one, been in the same
position, and they were able to offer me reassurance and
advice.'

So what is the advice?

- Some schools where there have been threatening incidents post notices warning of prosecution.

- Don't be caught behind your desk. Try to meet the complainer out in the entrance hall. (A head says, 'You're not normally caught out if everyone's alert and spots one of the usual suspects marching purposefully across the car park for example'.)

- Make sure another member of staff is with you, not as a bodyguard or to join in but to observe what happens.

- Speak firmly and clearly. Don't ask a furious person to calm down. It invariably make them worse. Say something more positive – 'Shall we talk about this or would you like to leave and come back when you're ready?'

- If the person is obviously worse for drink, don't engage with them at all. Insist they leave the building.

- If you're physically intimidated or assaulted, or if someone refuses to leave, ask the person with you to call the police.

- Write down details of any incident straight away while it's fresh in the mind.

- Always discuss a disturbing, threatening or violent incident, or a complaint against you or a colleague, with both the local authority and your professional association.

- If a colleague is threatened or assaulted, follow it up vigorously with the authority and, if necessary, with the police. Urge the colleague to contact his/her professional association.

■ Remember that an incident that seems to have gone away can resurface, perhaps as a formal accusation, and take you off guard. Be ready with evidence.

Give praise

If all this seems gloomy, then remember that if you have set up a reliable line of home–school communication, you can use it for good news as well as bad. Be generous and creative with letters of praise, certificates, warm words at the school gate.

Use the technology

Good management software is very valuable in enabling you to produce evidence of a child's performance, behaviour and attendance. Make sure you're using your MIS to the full as a home–school communication device.

Chapter 15

Relationship with the governors

The governors appointed you to the job and it wouldn't be natural if they didn't wonder, during the early days and weeks, how you were getting on.

That being so, it's possible that one or more of them – often, though not always, the chair – will take to dropping in unannounced 'Just to see how things are going.' Or it may be just that the chair had the habit of calling in at random moments during your predecessor's time.

Either way, if it happens – if the chair appears without warning, then you ought, quite early on, to take things in hand. The governors potentially have enormous powers, but once they've put you in charge of the school, they should abide by their decision and let you get on with it within clearly understood limits. You, for your part, need to be conscious of your status as head, which gives you the right to set boundaries around who comes into the building, and when.

■ Handling the casually visiting governor

The first time a governor comes into the school unannounced, gather them up from wherever they've landed – especially if it's a classroom – take them to your room, offer a cup of tea and ask directly what you can do to help. Have as friendly a conversation as necessary, answer questions. Whether you offer a walk around the school is up to you. When you're finished, establish that there's been an element of formality in the encounter by saying something like:

'Thank you for coming in. Governors are always welcome. Do you think you could give us a ring next time you want to come? There are times when we just can't give you as much attention as we'd like.'

If your visitor is the chair you could then say,

'I think it would be helpful if we set out at the governors' meeting a set of procedures for governors visiting the school. We want governor involvement, and it would be good to have it properly organised.'

▨ Organising governor involvement

It's actually up to the governors themselves to do this, but not all governing bodies will think of it, and in any case they will, or should, discuss the arrangements with you. So, just to help you prepare, here are some ideas that you, with your governors, can develop into a policy that suits your school.

▨ Specialist areas

It's a good idea for each governor to have a particular area of interest within the school. So, for example, there can be a governor for maths, another for literacy, another for special educational needs and so on. When this comes up for discussion, it's very important to emphasise that these roles do not call for any specialist subject knowledge. Be ready for the cries of of, 'Not maths! I was never any good at maths.'
So what does the subject governor do?

- ■ Gets to know the teacher in charge of the subject, mainly by sitting down and listening to him/her.

- ■ Becomes familiar with the way the subject is taught. (In sets? In mixed ability groups?)

- ■ Learns about resources for the subject – books, software, equipment.

■ Understands the school's performance in the subject.

■ Has a good knowledge of the challenges that face the subject leader.

■ Visits lessons in the subject, by arrangement, to look at areas which have been agreed in advance.

■ Works with the subject leader to prepare presentations on the subject to the governing body and/or parents' meetings.

■ Governors' visits

It's clear that most visits to the school by governors will take place within the framework of the governors' specialist interests. At the same time, there needs to be a general set of protocols for all governor visits.

There are lots of very good reasons why governors should visit school. Here are some of them:

■ to visit classrooms to see lessons

■ to talk to the administrator/finance officer

■ to meet with the head or other teachers

■ to look at the building for health and safety reasons, cleanliness, state of repair and so on

■ to become familiar with school equipment such as computers or science equipment.

BUT all of such visits should take place within a framework set down by the governing body as a whole, and with the knowledge and approval of the governing body.

This means:

■ a governor can't turn up unannounced and ask to see the accounts, to see a maths lesson or have a meeting with the deputy head.

■ no governor has any individual authority to make judgements based on observations and meetings. The governor's role is to report observations back to the governing body. So, for example, a governor can't watch a lesson then criticise it to the teacher, the head or anyone else.

■ visits should be planned within a programme which focuses on agreed areas. So, for example, if the governors have decided, with the head, to pay particular attention to maths during the Autumn term, then this decision will drive the schedule of governor visits.

Regular meetings with the chair

Many head teachers have weekly meetings with the chair, at scheduled times. There's nothing wrong with this, but bear in mind that for all practical purposes the chair really has no separate special status. It's sometimes difficult to convince the chair of this. In many cases he/she has assumed a unique status and the rest of the governors have just gone along with it. The truth is, though, that the chair is really just another governor. There are a few circumstances where the chair can take a decision that normally belongs to the governing body, but if you read the rules on this carefully you'll see that it's something that is hardly ever necessary. Even where a quick decision is needed, it's usually possible to call a short-notice meeting or at the very least share the responsibility with some phone calls. Too many governing bodies allow their chairs to 'take chair's action' in circumstances where it's neither necessary nor proper. Your job when that happens, even if it slows things down by a day or two, or causes you inconvenience, is to say, 'I think we should get the views of other governors.' It is not in your long-term interest or that of the school to see the chair dominating a governing body that, by its very nature, is made up of people with a range of interests and skills.

In the same way, don't work with the chair to 'fix' meetings in advance – or seem to do so. It's very off putting for the other governors if the head and the chair are obviously not only singing from the same hymn sheet but are doing a well-harmonised duet. It's quite natural in any organisation for pre-meeting lobbying and discussion to go on, but a good chair will actively solicit the views of other governors. If that

doesn't happen, then here too you must encourage it yourself.
'I wonder, Chair, whether we could hear what some of the other
governors have to say about this?'

Get to know all your governors

See your governors as a collection of people who are dedicated to the
school and want to support the children. Get to know them
individually, sound out their feelings about the school. Explore their
individual talents. Above all, encourage them to visit during the day,
and see what goes on. It's really not possible these days for a governor to
be effective if he/she doesn't visit the school during the working day,
and you may have to do some gentle persuasion. It helps if governors
realise just how children and teachers appreciate governors' visits – these
are people, after all, who make decisions affecting everyone who works
in the school.

Warning

Beware the 'Brother-in-law' approach. Sooner or later, when you're
considering having a job done in school – a building repair, electrical
work, a software upgrade – someone on the governing body or the PTA
will say something like, 'I can get you that done much more cheaply.
My brother-in-law. . . .'

Even if it's legal – which it often isn't, in the sense of being in breach
of the authority's rules – getting work done in that way invariably leads
to tears. What you have to realise, though, is that there's a whole section
of society who live their lives on that kind of personal contact, and you
may find it difficult to persuade some governors that it can't happen.

Chapter 16
Adopting and enjoying the role

We've already said that as a new head, you're on a different planet. And if you visit a different planet, then you need to dress and behave appropriately. Lose your protective clothing and you're in trouble. In this case, the clothing is mainly, though not entirely, metaphorical. What we're actually discussing is the importance of assuming the role of leader – acting as if you're in charge, believing it and relishing it. The soccer manager Lawrie McMenemy who (many of you will be pleased to know) led Southampton to victory over Manchester United in the 1976 FA Cup Final, once said in an interview on leadership,

> *The first thing you must do when you walk through the door is take charge. Then, every morning after that, look in the mirror and ask yourself, "Do I want to be in charge?" If the answer is not an immediate yes, then get out.*
>
> (Brady and Bolchover 2004)

That's not bad advice for a head teacher. Right from the start of your headship, people will assume that you are in charge. How you respond to that is crucial. And yet in a sense it's simple – you respond by actually taking charge.

That sounds obvious, but it needs to be said, because in fact it's very easy to be mesmerised by the attention to the point where you bask in it and forget to go out and actively be the leader.

All the obvious notes of caution are true of course. We've dealt already with the importance of listening and thinking, and how it's not necessary or desirable to make autocratic edicts just to show who's boss.

Neither, though, is it right to be listening and thinking so hard that you seem to your colleagues to be doing nothing at all. But the very act of listening can show that you're in charge. If you say, decisively, something like

> *I'm going to meet with each one of you privately over the next week or two. I want to get to know you. More importantly I want you to get to know me, and have the opportunity to tell me how we can best work together for our children'*

then you're saying, 'I'm in charge,' just as effectively – more so in fact – than if you were to put out a pompous memo asking people not to park in your space.

In the end, it's all about the quality that we call 'the air of authority'. If you have it, then you'll enjoy the job.

This isn't, by the way, some vague attribute that you have to be born with. Much is written about the importance, in leadership, of personality. What's not so often said is that the key lies not in what you're like but in what you do. It's your actions that make you a good leader or a bad one, and that will win you either respect or indifference.

So let's say again – regardless of how you feel inside, or how nervous you are – the things you do and say must mark you out as the person in charge. It's to do, for example, with appearing confident and comfortable in any setting. If you walk into a room carrying the expectation that people will stop and take notice of you, then they probably will. Your aim is that anyone encountering a gathering of your staff would immediately identify you as the head teacher. One successful head describes this as, 'reassuring the parents and governors by your manner and presence that they're getting value for money'.

■ The first day

In a sense, you'll have more than one 'first day'. You'll probably be seen around the school, and have some meetings, before you formally take up your appointment. Then you may well have a teacher training day ahead of the arrival of the children. Even so, that actual first 'live' day with the children in school is a crucial one – the first time that most of your community of children and adults have seen you in action as the person in charge.

Try hard to be very visible on that first day. Don't get stuck in your room. Arrive in school very early, walk the building and stop to talk to anyone you meet – teachers, caretaker, children dropped off by their parents. In a big school, with a lot of people around, you might like to consider wearing a name badge. Use your judgement as to whether that's a step too far. If you do wear a badge, make it a good-quality one,

As the flood of arrivals increases, try to spend some time at the main gate if you can, but certainly in the entrance hall. By now you should know the names of your staff – that's quite a challenge, but a good secretary will have helped you with this before you started – and you'll be greeting them personally as they arrive.

It's useful to have a morning briefing session for the whole staff 10 minutes before school starts, and on your first day it may be the first time you've met them en masse in a formal setting. Be businesslike and to the point. Of course you'll comment on the fact that it's your first day and that you look forward to working with everyone, but this is not an occasion for speeches. Don't be apologetic, don't make weak jokes. Very quickly hand over to your deputy for announcements.

Your first assembly is important. Decide how you want it to start. Do you want your deputy to settle everyone down before you come in? Or do you want to be at the front when everyone enters? Take account of established practice, and maybe go along with it on your first morning – but don't be afraid to change it quickly afterwards. If you feel you can't live with the existing system, then let staff know and change it the very next day. It's one of those areas where you can make your mark very early on.

Try to run the first assembly as if you've been doing them for ages. (You'll need to talk to the deputy about this in advance.) So if there are awards to give out, or announcements to make, just get on and do them. You'll introduce yourself, of course, and say, briefly, that you're looking forward to meeting everyone. Say that you're looking to see everyone try hard with their work and behaviour, and that you have high expectations. Don't be afraid to tackle the child who shows off, giggling with a friend – the hard stare, the pause and, perhaps, 'Did you understand that?' will be enough.

Spend a lot of time around the building as the day goes on. At break and lunchtime spend time with the staff on duty. Visit the canteen staff and the lunchtime supervisors. Consider eating with the children – you'll want to do this at times, but perhaps on the first day you'll want to be on your feet for the whole of the lunch hour. It's quite likely, though, that the kitchen staff or the children will ask you to have lunch, in which case it would be churlish to refuse.

Get around into the far-flung corners of the building and surroundings at lunchtime. Stop to talk to children and adults. Don't forget, though, to visit the staffroom and have coffee or tea with the staff. Regard yourself as a visitor to the staffroom. Wait to be invited to take coffee and to sit down. If the invitation doesn't come, say, 'May I have a coffee please?', 'May I sit here for a moment?' Don't stay for the whole break though. As time goes on you'll probably begin to feel entirely comfortable in the staffroom. It's important, though, always to see yourself as a visitor, and to allow staff plenty of time to themselves.

At the end of the day, go out to the gate, speak to the children as they leave and, importantly, chat to the parents who are waiting there. They'll know who you are, but it's still polite to introduce yourself, and this also gives you the opportunity to ask one or two of them their names, and who their children are. Try not to get drawn into deep conversations about individual children, but do say, 'Don't hesitate to come and see me if you have any worries.'

In encounters like this, try to see yourself not just as the parents see you but as the parents want to see you. On the whole they want you to be approachable and smiling. But they also want you to look smart, to be authoritative and to induce just a slight feeling of awe. Remember that parents are thinking of you as the person looking after their children, and that means they want you to be caring, bright, kind – and a stickler for correct behaviour and hard work. Try to see yourself like that. Act the part.

■ Remember Lawrie

Above all, remember Lawrie McMenemy. In all that you do in those early hours and days, act as if you are quietly, unostentatiously, but unmistakably, in charge. Small things can make a difference. Here's a head recalling that first day.

> 'When I took over, the school had a system called "The Book". It was really a handwritten, daily diary, in an A4, hardback notebook, containing the sort of announcements that in some schools are written up on a whiteboard in the staffroom. There'd be the date, then underneath entries about staff absence, visitors, changes to timetable and so on. The deputy head wrote it up every morning well before school. It was her baby. She circulated it among the staff and everyone initialled it. Should she continue doing it, she asked. "Of course", I said.
>
> On the first morning, before school, she told me she'd done The Book, and was about to start circulating it.
>
> "No", I said. "Leave it with me and collect it in a few minutes."
>
> I read her entries, added a couple of things of my own, made a note to query later some of the things she'd written and then called her in to hand it back.
>
> What I'd done, of course – and I promise I didn't realise it at the time – was accomplish the trick of taking ownership of this procedure (The Book was a powerful symbol in the school, anything that wasn't in it didn't exist) without undermining the deputy. Some months later, she said to me, "It was that first morning, when you asked me for The Book, that I knew we had a different sort of head".'

■ First meeting

At some point at the beginning of your headship – perhaps on the first day – will come the moment when you stand up before the staff and introduce yourself. It's a key event, and you need to think about it and get the tone and the content right. Here's what one head teacher said (maybe not word for word, but the gist is right). We've added some comments.

'My name's Sam Wilson. I was a class teacher for six years and deputy head for seven years. Now I'm proud to be head teacher here at Marmalade Road Primary.'

(Sam emphasises here that she's done her classroom time, following the same path as the people to whom she's speaking. But she doesn't name the schools she's been in – she's looking forward not back.)

'I've always wanted to be a head, and having achieved that, my next ambition is to serve this school and its children successfully and well, and I can't do that without your help and support.'

(The word 'serve' is important here, as is the early mention of children.)

'You gave that support in full measure to my predecessor, and I know, because she told me herself, how much she appreciated it.'

(It's good to pay a tribute to your predecessor. In all but the direst circumstances you can find something positive to say. Here, Sam subtly indicates that the two have discussed the staff.)

'I ask you, quite frankly and openly, for the same support – though I know well that as time goes on you will expect me to earn it, and to show that it's being repaid in full measure.'

(You can – using diplomatic language – actually demand support, provided you make clear your intention also to earn it.)

'Of course I have ideas and plans and a determination to go forward.'

(I'm in charge.)

'But I also have a listening ear, because you have ideas and plans too,

rooted in a deeper understanding than mine of this community and its children.'

(Flattery never does any harm. But make sure you mean this, because if you don't, they'll see right through you.)

'So we need each other. We'll agree at times. We'll disagree at others. We may even have some fun.'

(The last comment, delivered with a smile, is intended to lighten the atmosphere. It's the nearest thing you should get to a joke.)

'But we won't ever forget why we're here, which is to carry forward the deeply serious business of increasing the life chances of our children. Let nothing get in the way of that.'

(The phrase 'increasing the life chances' is recommended as a good and broader alternative to 'improving achievement' or 'raising standards'.)

Dos and don'ts about first meetings with the staff and, where appropriate, with the parents

Do:

- Look the part. Stand still and proud. Smile, make eye contact around the room. Pause occasionally and smile warmly at someone who looks serious until he/she smiles back.

- Be brief. The first introduction is not a time for laying out detailed plans.

- Pay a brief tribute to your predecessor.

- Pay a similar tribute to the staff for their work. If there's been a success – good Ofsted, Investors In People – give praise.

Don't:

■ Mention your previous school. Your colleagues – and you yourself if it comes to that – need to be reassured that you're looking forward and not back.

■ Make jokes. It's the area most likely to trap you into sounding false, forced or insensitive. A joke that doesn't work is a hundred times worse than no joke at all.

■ Apologise. Never say things like, 'Of course I'm very much a learner here . . .' or, 'You probably don't realise it but I'm pretty nervous . . .'. To put it bluntly, you're being paid not to feel like that.

Chapter 17

The support of colleagues – and the kindness of friends

Everyone says that headship is a lonely job. You can see why. It's rarely that you can let your hair down and have a moan about a colleague. Of course, you can always go home, throw your bag down, kick the cat and say, 'I'll kill that literacy co-ordinator one day, so help me!' But your partner will very quickly inform you that this isn't the relationship he/she signed up for.

Some heads develop a close relationship with their chair of governors. Even that, though, can – or should – only go so far. The governors are directly responsible for the efficiency of the school, and that means they have to monitor how well you are managing things. So if you take the opportunity to complain too strongly, you may simply be giving out the message that you haven't got a proper grip.

Much the same goes for local authority advisers, whose role is fast changing. Once, the adviser could be a confidante and friend. A head recalls,

> 'When a neighbouring head, a close friend, died suddenly in post, the adviser came straight out to see me. I broke down and cried as she spoke to me. I can't see anything like that happening now. I'm not always certain that people at the local authority are sure which of us is still alive.'

So to a certain extent the loneliness is inevitable, and you have to accept it. After all, headship isn't unique in that – lots of top jobs are hedged around in the same way. You could argue, in fact, that heads are slightly more fortunate than many other leaders because, at least, there isn't as much competitiveness and backbiting as there is in some other walks of life. Heads do, at least, talk to each other, and that, in the end, is what helps with the loneliness. We're not like leaders in industry who daren't share problems for fear of betraying secrets.

A head tells a story of an industrial placement:

> *'I went to a car parts firm for a fortnight. One day I was sitting*
> *with a human resources officer as she struggled to fill in a big*
> *government form. She was having real trouble understanding an*
> *important part of it. Every HR department, she said, had to do this*
> *particular form every year. Why then, I wondered, did she not just*
> *phone up a more experienced counterpart in another firm and ask*
> *for help?*
>
> *She looked at me as if I'd gone mad. Under no circumstances could*
> *one firm help another, even with something that had no bearing at*
> *all on the core business. It was an eye-opening moment. The contrast*
> *with the way we behave in school couldn't have been more stark. I*
> *remember as a new head battling with forms and returns all of*
> *which were then done manually. I had bags of help from the*
> *experienced heads in the town. I only had to phone one of them.'*

That's right isn't it? Heads are excellent networkers. This is particularly true of primary heads, because the schools are smaller and closer together. In any urban area there'll be a dozen primaries whose heads are all known to each other at least by name and by sight.

So, never underestimate the desire of your fellow heads to help you. You are not in the kind of business where people want to see you fail. Every head remembers the early days, and most are ready to work through them with you. As time goes on, you'll soon discover the true 'gurus' – the heads who have a real commitment to the local head teacher community. Sometimes they're active in a professional association, but that's not always the case. Often they're just helpful folk. They know what works with difficult parents or broken heating systems. They can tell you who to talk to at the office. Most importantly, they can advise you how to protect yourself against the effects of your own ill-advised decisions.

If the local heads have meetings – whether as an official group or just as an informal 'mafia' – always try to attend. You'll be made welcome and you'll learn the real story as opposed to the official one from the authority.

▨ Partners and mentors

In many authorities, new heads are put into a formal mentoring partnership with an experienced colleague. It's an excellent scheme, and although you'd think there'd be times when the people didn't hit it off, it hardly ever seems to happen. There's usually a generosity of spirit and a constant awareness of the underlying purpose, which is to make things better for children. That's invariably enough to keep partnerships focussed on what they have in common rather than on any philosophical differences or soccer team rivalries.

A head says:

> *'My mentor was brilliant. She was very supportive, and would always return calls, ready to talk things through. She could see any flaws in my ideas and she'd talk me through them. She was very up to date on all the paperwork things we had to do.*
>
> *She had two people to mentor, and the three of us would have regular evenings out, or lunches. Now I'm beyond the first year I regard it as important to keep that going, and for us to make time for each other. This is a lonely job – you can't just talk to anybody in the school about your feelings, and it's good to have two others to share things with you.'*

Making the best of the relationship means not being afraid to ask for help. There are lots of times when a new head faces something – anything from a sentence in an official document, to an acronym thrown out in a meeting, to an urgent query from a parent or a member of staff – that he/she feels they ought to know the meaning of. That's when it's time to throw away all inhibitions and ask. If you're in the meeting, put your hand up. If it's in a document, or if it's a query from a member of staff, phone somebody. Just don't be afraid, ever, to ask.

Here's another head.

> *'In the early days of special needs legislation, I was in a meeting of heads and chairs of governors at which all the new regulations were being explained. The person doing the presentation kept using the word, "Senco" as an abbreviation for Special Educational Needs Co-ordinator. Now, of course, we all use the word. Then, it was new, and not everyone knew it, so it was naughty of the presenter to assume that we all did. We all meekly continued to listen in ignorance, however, until eventually one chair of governors had the courage and the wit to put up her hand and ask what this strange word meant. The relief all around the room was palpable.'*

And that's how it usually is. However obvious and simple the question is, you're not the only one who wants to know. Even the expert you phone may have to confess the need to ask someone else. And it's actually quite a good idea to ask even if you think you know the answer.

> *'It proves you're human for one thing, and you can get a different insight into things from someone who's had more experience of how things pan out. I have a good network now of heads I can talk to.'*

Epilogue
Random point winners

- Be around the building, talking, watching, listening.

- Know as many names as possible.

- Keep to commitments – if you've promised to see a lesson, see it. If you've arranged to see parents, see them. If you've promised to ring the office on somebody's behalf, do it.

- Have recruitment permanently in mind – keep an eye open for promising teachers everywhere:
  - when you visit other schools (you won't poach, but you might talk to the head to see whether someone wants a move)
  - when you have students in on school experience
  - at combined school events – music festivals, sports meetings.

- Don't be Mr Perkupp. He's the chief clerk who, in George and Weedon Grossmith's *Diary of a Nobody* tells Mr Pooter he wants to see him about something important and then keeps him waiting for three days on tenterhooks because he's too busy.

- Be the head – bearing, dress, body language, speech.

- Preserve some space around you. Don't be too cosy with staff, governors or parents.

- Keep teaching and learning as the focus of meetings and policies. Make a point of discussing a child-centred issue at every staff meeting.

- Always be conscious of keeping your children safe. Never stop looking at such things as police-check documents, procedures for tracking attendance, security of external doors, possibility of internal truancy, places and occasions where bullying might happen, procedure for admitting visitors, routines for handing children over to parents and family.

- Give your staff the best possible working conditions.

- Beware of subconsciously showing favouritism towards some members of staff.

- Always appear calm and unruffled. Soak up your colleagues' worries, and don't transmit yours to them.

- For the sake of your peace of mind, be aware of when you need another person in the room during an interview with children or a family. Or, alternatively, be prepared to carry out an interview in an open area with people passing by. A retired head says,

  'Towards the end of my career, when we were becoming more conscious of such things, I would often use the comfortable chairs in the entrance hall for interviews, with the door open on to the secretary's room.'

- When the day of multiple and challenging problems comes along (severe weather, flood, fire) remember that once all the children are accounted for, safe and supervised, everything else can be dealt with methodically in order.

- Guard against off-the-cuff remarks that can be magnified in importance by the people listening. ('I really can't stand people who. . . .')

- Don't hog the conversation in the staffroom. You may be abusing the fact that people feel obliged to listen to you.

- Let people do their jobs.

- Protect your colleagues from abusive or violent behaviour by parents and other visitors.

- Support your colleagues in public to the absolute limit of what's ethical and legal.

- Keep your values to the forefront – always be ready to ask, 'Are we a school that does this sort of thing?'

- Support out-of-school activities by turning up to them and talking to people.

- Attend staff social events. Don't spend all evening with your deputy. Know when to leave.

- Correct or reprimand staff in private.

- Don't complain about your health. Either shut up or go home.

- Thank people. Write notes or cards of appreciation every day.

- Take an interest in your colleagues' families. Make a fuss of their children and babies when you meet them.

- If and when you meet the parents of your younger teachers, be very warm and courteous towards them. They are infinitely proud of their offspring.

- Don't put down a colleagues' choice of entertainment. ('You don't really like Barry Manilow do you?')

- Beware of corridor or staffroom encounters with colleagues and then forgetting what was said. If it seems that the conversation is becoming important, cut it short and ask the colleague to come and see you, or write a note. But don't forget, else you'll get a reputation for being dismissive of colleagues' concerns.

- Enjoy the job. Take time to realise how fortunate you are to spend your working days in the company of young people.

Final word

A retired head says,

> 'My most cherished memory is of the end of the Christmas play,
> which always finished with a traditional nativity scene. I'd walk
> forward and sit on the edge of the low stage to say a few words. The
> children would be all close around me, many in the familiar nativity
> play costumes, and often one would quite naturally put a hand on
> my shoulder. The hall was always packed, with people standing
> round the sides and at the back. I'd tell the parents how I felt – what
> a precious thing it was for me to have this kind of Christmas. And
> really the memory is so clear that I still do have it really.'

References

Gerstner, L. V. (2002) *Who Says Elephants Can't Dance?* New York: HarperCollins.

Brady, C. and Bolchover, D. (2004) *The 90-Minute Manager: Lessons from the Sharp End of Management.* Prentice-Hall.

Index